the CENTER for

heRmeneutícaL studíes

in HELLENISTIC and MODERN CULTURE

he GRADUATE THEOLOGICAL UNION & The UNIVERSITY of CALIFORNIA

BERKELEY, CALIFORNIA

PROTOCOL OF THE THIRTY-NINTH COLLOQUY: 26 MAY 1980

INTERPRETATION, META-INTERPRETATION, AND OEDIPUS TYRANNUS

BARRIE A. WILSON
PROFESSOR OF PHILOSOPHY
YORK UNIVERSITY, DOWNSVIEW, ONTARIO, CANADA

IRENE LAWRENCE, *Editor*

ISSN   0098-0900

Key title:
Protocol of the colloquy of the Center for Hermeneutical Studies
in Hellenistic and Modern Culture

Library of Congress Cataloging in Publication Data

Center for Hermeneutical Studies in Hellenistic
    and Modern Culture.
    Interpretation, meta-interpretation, and Oedipus   *PA*
tyrannus.
                                                        4413
    (Protocol series of the colloquies of the Center
; 39 ISSN 0098-0900)   *.07*
    "Select bibliography of Barrie A. Wilson" : p.
    1. Sophocles. Oedipus tyrannus--Congresses.   *C46*
I. Wilson Barrie A.   II. Lawrence, Irene, 1942-
III. Title.   IV. Series: Center for Hermeneutical   *1980*
Studies in Hellenistic and Modern Culture. Protocol
series of the colloquies ; 39.
PA4413.07C46 1980   882'.01   80-28919
ISBN 0-89242-038-3

Published by

The CENTER FOR HERMENEUTICAL STUDIES in
Hellenistic and Modern Culture

2465 Le Conte Avenue
Berkeley, CA   94709
USA

TABLE OF CONTENTS

Barrie A. Wilson
INTERPRETATION, META-INTERPRETATION, AND OEDIPUS TYRANNUS   1-28

RESPONSES

    Bryant Keeling, *Professor of Philosophy*   29-31
    Western Illinois University, Macomb, Illinois

    Hans Ulrich Gumbrecht, *Professor of Romance Literature*   32-34
    University of the Ruhr, Bochum, West Germany
    Visiting Professor of French, University of California, Berkeley

    Marvin Brown, *Lecturer in Religion and Society*   35-36
    Graduate Theological Union, Berkeley

    Joseph Fontenrose, *Professor of Classics, Emeritus*   37-40
    University of California, Berkeley

    Mark Griffith, *Associate Professor of Classics*   41-46
    University of California, Berkeley

MINUTES OF THE COLLOQUY

    List of Participants   47

    The Discussion   48-

SELECT BIBLIOGRAPHY OF BARRIE A. WILSON

INTERPRETATION, META-INTERPRETATION, AND OEDIPUS TYRANNUS

BARRIE A. WILSON

> Misguided men! What is this foolish war of words
> You have raised?
> >   (*Oedipus Tyrannus, ll.*633,634)

I

It is one thing to interpret a text; it is quite another matter to offer an account of textual interpretation. The first has been called "exegesis," that is, the giving of an interpretation to a text by an interpreter. I shall call this activity, "interpretation." The second has been called "hermeneutics," that is, a view, theory, or account of what constitutes an interpretation or an understanding of a text.[1] This activity represents the development of a view *about* interpretation, and, as such, is an inquiry at the meta-level. I shall call this second inquiry, "meta-interpretation."

Often the exegetical approach adopted by an interpreter discloses an assumed hermeneutic stance, for there is a close connection between the fruits of interpretation and the meta-interpretative method employed. Yet rarely do interpreters offer interpretation and meta-interpretation in one and the same study.

Bernard M. W. Knox, however, represents an exception to this. In *Oedipus at Thebes*[2] Knox presents an interpretation of Sophocles' *Oedipus Tyrannus*. It is a systematic, well argued, and provocative interpretation, one that basically views the play as advocating a return to traditional Greek religion and an abandonment of a form of scientific humanism that was becoming popular in the Athens of Sophocles' time.

In presenting this interpretation, Knox also seeks to support and exemplify a specific meta-interpretative position. As he says,

> This book is essentially a study of the Sophoclean play, *Oedipus Tyrannus*, in terms of the age which produced it, an attempt to answer the question, "What did it mean to them, there, then?" But it suggests also an answer to the question, "What does it mean to us, here, now?" And the answer suggested is: the same thing it meant to them, there, then. (pp. 1, 2)

A meta-interpretative position that unabashedly emphasizes that interpretation involves recapturing what it meant to them, there, then seems an ambitious if not impossible project, especially in the light of the contentions of the Heideggerian-style hermeneutics

---

[1]For a discussion of different conceptions of hermeneutics, see Richard E. Palmer, *Hermeneutics* (Evanston: Northwestern University Press 1969) chaps. 3 & 5.

[2]Bernard M. W. Knox, *Oedipus at Thebes* (New York: W. W. Norton 1971). All subsequent references to this work (first published in 1957 by Yale University Press) will be to the Norton edition and will be placed in parentheses following the quoted or referred to material.

2

now currently in vogue. Meta-interpretative theorists such as Bultmann,[3] Gadamer,[4] and
many others[5] have attempted to work out the implications of historicity for textual understanding and their results would appear to raise serious doubts concerning the feas-
ibility of Knox's project.

At the same time, Knox does not advocate the meta-interpretative alternative to
Heideggerian hermeneutics as proposed by Hirsch,[6] namely one that seeks to recover the
author's intended meaning as the meaning of the text. In pursuing his meta-interpretative objectives, Knox does not speculate on nor does he try to establish Sophocles' intended meaning in the play. Rather he carefully examines the text itself, situating it
in the context of movements in the age in which the play was performed in order to arrive
at an understanding of what it means.

In explicitly bringing to the fore the question of what the text meant to them
there, then, Knox is putting forward a view which essentially represents a third meta-
interpretative option. This option, which might be dubbed a "hermeneutics of fidelity,"
is one that focusses on the text of the play itself and its meaning in the context of
its original production. Coming as it does from classical scholarship, this view is
interestingly paralleled in New Testament scholarship in the writings of Oscar Cullmann
who, like Knox, is both a hermeneut as well as an exegete. Cullmann, for instance, contends:

---

[3]The following works by Rudolf Bultmann are pertinent in this respect: "New
Testament and Mythology," in H. W. Bartsch (ed.), *Kerygma and Myth*, I (London: S.P.C.
1964) 1-44; "The Problem of Hermeneutics," in R. Bultmann, *Essays Philosophical and
Theological* (London: SCM Press 1955) 234-261; *Jesus Christ and Mythology* (New York:
Scribner's 1958); and "Is Exegesis without Presuppositions Possible?" in *Existence and
Faith: Shorter Writings of Rudolf Bultmann*, trans. Schubert M. Ogden (New York: World
1960). For a critical discussion of Bultmann's position, see, for instance, the au-
thor's "Bultmann's Hermeneutics: A Critical Examination," *International Journal for
Philosophy of Religion* 8 (1977) 169-189.

[4]See, for instance, the following works by Hans-Georg Gadamer: *Le Problème
de la Conscience Historique* (Paris: Béatrice-Nauwelaerts 1963); *Truth and Method* (New
York: Seabury 1975. Originally published as *Wahrheit und Methode*, Tübingen 1965); and
Philosophical Hermeneutics (Berkeley and Los Angeles: University of California Press
1976).

[5]Among a great many authors, the now classic works of Dilthey, Heidegger, and
Ebeling should especially be mentioned. See also R. E. Palmer, *op. cit.*; Robert R.
Maglioloa, *Phenomenology and Literature* (West Lafayette: Purdue University Press
1977); and David Couzens Hoy, *The Critical Circle* (Berkeley and Los Angeles: University of California Press 1978).

[6]See E. D. Hirsch, Jr., *Validity in Interpretation* (New Haven: Yale University Press 1967), and *Aims of Interpretation* (Chicago: University of Chicago Press
1976). For a critical discussion of Hirsch's position, see, for instance, the author's
"Hirsch's Hermeneutics: A Critical Examination," *Philosophy Today* 22 (1978) 20-33.

I emphasize here only that I know no other "method" than the proven philolog-
ical-historical one. I know of no other "attitude" toward the text than obe-
dient willingness to listen to it even when what I hear is sometimes completely
foreign, contradictory to my own favorite ideas, whatever they may be....[7]

and in this Cullmann is espousing a hermeneutics of fidelity.

Is it possible to steer a hermeneutic course between the Charybdis of historicity (and its alleged implications for understanding) on the one hand and the Scylla
of the author's intended meaning as constitutive of the text's correct meaning on the
other? In other words, is a third meta-interpretative option possible?

It would be an enormous undertaking, of course, to attempt to construct a hermeneutics of fidelity to the text. Much remains unclear about the nature of textual
interpretation at both the interpretative and meta-interpretative levels. I shall not
attempt such a construction. There are, however, several preliminary and prior matters that need to be probed much more closely before such a construction could be attempted. These matters I will examine.

In this paper I am concerned with two main questions, one at the level of interpretation and one at the meta-interpretative level. I use the former to open up the
latter, it being my conviction that interpretation has (or ought to have) an important
bearing on meta-interpretation. At the level of interpretation I ask, of a particular
text, (I) what does it mean? The text I have selected for interpretative scrutiny is
Sophocles' *Oedipus Tyrannus*.[8] I examine various attempts to answer this question with
respect to this text, and, in so doing, I sketch the outlines of a major interpretative
controversy. Section II of this paper examines Knox's interpretation of the play; section III then presents several quite different understandings of the play, at least one
of them being incompatible with Knox's interpretation.

I start with a particular interpretative controversy chiefly for two main reasons. First of all, it is out of a heterogeneity of meanings that question (I) takes
on a problematic status. Secondly, I find that there are certain facets of the controversial nature of textual interpretation that suggest a direction for meta-interpretative reflection, facets which have been largely overlooked hitherto.

In attempting to answer question (I), I find a great variety of responses, some
of them incompatible with one another. I then move (in section IV of this paper) to
ask a different sort of question, namely, (II) what are we to make of the situation
whereby question (I) receives as an answer that the text has been given a variety of

---

[7]Oscar Cullmann, *The Christology of the New Testament* (Philadelphia: Westmin-
ster 1959) xiv. See also "Les problèmes posés par la méthode exégetique de l'école de
Karl Barth," *Revue d'Histoire et de Philosophie Religieuses* 8 (1928) 70-83.

[8]It should be pointed out here that I am not a classics scholar but rather a
philosopher interested in the works of classical antiquity. In my study of the play
I have consulted the following: F. Storr (trans.), *Sophocles: Oedipus the King* (Lon-
don: William Heinemann, Loeb Classical Library 1912); Bernard M. W. Knox, *op. cit.*;
Thomas Gould (trans., with commentary), *Sophocles, Oedipus the King* (Englewood Cliffs:
Prentice-Hall 1970); Luci Berkowitz and Theodore F. Brunner (trans., ed.), *Sophocles,
Oedipus Tyrannus* (New York: W. W. Norton 1970); and Philip Vellacott, *Sophocles and
Oedipus* (Ann Arbor: University of Michigan Press 1971).

different interpretations? In the light of a meta-interpretative direction that grow
out of noting certain facets of interpretative controversy, I examine (in section V
this paper) various aspects of question (II). I point out the pentadic structure of
textual interpretation, the importance for meta-interpretation of a study of interpre
tative arguments, and I suggest a way in which a logic of textual interpretation cou'
be developed. In this way some problematic features of questions (I) and (II) are
opened up and clarified.

In sum this paper sets out to do three things: (a) to present an interpretative controversy, (b) to examine the theoretical import of the sort of interpretative
controversy that results in interpretative diversity (and incompatibility), and (c) t
suggest a new meta-interpretative direction, one that arises from the controversial r
ture of textual interpretation itself and which emphasizes the central role of interp
tative arguments.

Before venturing into meta-interpretation, let us begin by focussing on the i
terpretation of one particular text, namely Sophocles' *Oedipus Tyrannus*, and let us a
in all naivete, what does it mean?

II

Knox presents the following argument in support of his interpretation of *Oedi
Tyrannus*. For ease of reference subsequently, the argument will be referred to as "a
gument A" and the main points will be numbered and referred to as "A-claims":

A1. In the play, Oedipus' will is free. (pp. 5,12)

Knox rejects the popular interpretative view that the play is a tragedy of fate. Indeed, he claims, "in the actions of Oedipus in the play 'fate' plays no part at all"
(p. 6). Knox is aware, of course, that this view is highly controversial and he is c
ful to consider, and subsequently reject, three possible counterclaims to A1.

For one thing, early on in the play, Tiresias announces in his presence that
Oedipus murdered Laius. He also predicts both Oedipus' discovery and blindness. It
might be argued, on this basis, that the play is therefore a fulfillment of this prop
ecy and a demonstration of the power and truth of fate.

Knox rejects this construal. Tiresias' utterance, he points out, is not an e
ternal force operating on Oedipus. Tiresias speaks, but only under duress, against h
firm resolve not to speak, and in response to Oedipus' provocation. It is, moreover,
without effect: Tiresias' prophetic utterance has no effect, Knox contends, on Oedipus' subsequent action. His prophecy thus does not make anything happen.

Secondly, Knox points out that Tiresias explicitly says, "No--it is not I who will ca
your fall. That is Apollo's office--and he will discharge it" (*ll.* 376, 377). Here
Oedipus' downfall is specifically attributed to the causal agency of Apollo. On this
basis it might be argued that Oedipus' catastrophe is simply the result of divine activity.

Again Knox rejects this construal. He points out that modern translations of
this passage depend on a 1786 emendation of the text by Brunck, noting that the original text states in effect, "if I am to fall, that is Apollo's business and he can tak
care of it" (p. 8). Knox also adds that an emendation ought not to be accepted unless
the original does not make sense which, in this case, it does.

Thirdly, Knox observes that

it might also be urged that the process of Oedipus' self-discovery starts with
his request to the Delphic oracle for advice about the plague, that the plague
is therefore the causal factor, and the plague is sent by Apollo, who in this
play represents the external factor, "fate." (pp. 8, 9)

There is no suggestion, however, as Knox points out, that Apollo is responsible for the
plague. Apollo's priest prays at the outset for Apollo to rescue the city from the
plague but he does not thereby connect Apollo with having caused the plague in the beginning. The Chorus, moreover, attributes the plague to Ares and regards Apollo, along
with Athena, Artemis, and Dionysus as allies in the struggle. The plague, therefore,
is not the manifestation of fate. That there is an initial plague is, however, important, for it represents a problem that prompts Oedipus into action.

Not only are Oedipus' actions not presented by Sophocles as fated, they are,
on the contrary, presented as stemming from a decisive man of action, a person who is
clearly capable of thinking for himself and of making decisions. He decides, for instance, to hear Creon's report from the oracle in public; he decides to search for the
murderer of Laius; he decides, even before the Chorus suggests it, to consult Tiresias;
he decides, moreover, to proceed with the investigation even though counselled four
times against doing so. Oedipus is free, not fated.

This has important consequences for the development of the plot. As Knox points
out, "Oedipus' action is not only the action of a free agent, it is also the cause of
the events of the play" (p. 12). The events that take place in the play occur because
of Oedipus' actions. It is his relentless pursuit of the truth, and the decisions he
makes along the way, that set in motion and sustain the plot. So, in addition to Al,
Knox also contends:

A2. The decisions and actions of Oedipus are the causal factors in
the plot of the tragedy. (p. 14)

Not only that, but Knox also maintains:

A3. These decisions and actions are the expression of the character of
Oedipus. (p. 14)

What, then, is the character of Oedipus? Knox discusses this at length (pp. 14-29),
essentially portraying him as a man of decision and action. Oedipus reflects, delib-
erates, and interrogates. Three times he skilfully examines a witness (Creon, the messenger from Corinth, the shepherd). He demands a rational basis for his beliefs, coun-
tenancing, Knox points out, "no mysteries, no half-truths, no half-measures" (p. 18).
He is by no means portrayed as a passive pawn in the operations of a relentless fate.

Knox asks, "From what aspects or aspect of the hero's character do the decisive
actions spring?" (p. 29). He locates it precisely on "his intelligence, which will accept nothing incomplete, nothing untested, only the full truth" (p. 30). As Knox points
out, Oedipus refuses to accept Tiresias' insistence that he drop the whole matter; he
refuses to accept Jocasta's plea to be satisfied with the situation; and he again refuses to accept Jocasta's suggestion to let matters lie following the arrival of the
Corinthian messenger. In each case Oedipus presses on with the inquiry. Here, says
Knox, "he is most himself" (p. 30). It is on this basis that Knox makes the following
claim:

A4. The catastrophe of Oedipus is a product not of any one quality
of Oedipus but of the total man. (p. 31)

The actions that occur in the play come about not because of any one flaw in the mak
up of Oedipus (and it is here, on the basis of A4, that Knox rejects Aristotle's int
pretation of the play) but rather because Oedipus as a whole is the sort of person h
is. There is catastrophe in the play, to be sure, but it is one that shocks the rea
or hearer because of its enormity, not because it is linked to any *hamartia* in the ch
cter of Oedipus.

The meaning of the play, therefore, does not lie in the role of fate (A1 pre
cludes this) nor does it lie in any one fatal flaw inherent in Oedipus' character (p
cluded by A4). Where, then, is the meaning of the play to be found?

It is clear *what* Oedipus learns in the course of the play. As Knox points o

What he discovers in the play is not only that he is his father's murderer and
his mother's husband, but that he has long ago fulfilled to the letter the pre-
diction which he thought he had so far dodged, and which, at the height of his
hope, he thought he had escaped forever. (p. 33)

This directs our attention to an element outside Oedipus' decisions and actions whic
also plays a significant role in the play: the role of prophecy. The actions whose
true nature Oedipus comes eventually to understand have been predicted. They had be
predicted to Laius and then to Oedipus as a youth.

That the major events in Oedipus' life had been predicted must be carefully
derstood. This is not to say, as Knox is at pains to point out, that Oedipus' actio
are in any sense caused by divine agency:

...in the *Œdipus Tyrannus* Sophocles has chosen to present the terrible actions
of Oedipus not as determined but only as predicted, and he has made no reference to the relation between the predicted destiny and the divine will. (p. 38)

Nor is it to say that prophecy and prophecy alone is the causal agency at work in th
play. Rather the plot is much more complicated and subtle, for it is the combinatio
of prophecy along with, and in interaction with, Oedipus' character that eventually
produces the outcome.

According to Knox, the meaning of the play is therefore to be located in the
complex interaction between prophecy and Oedipus' character. Specifically it is to
found in terms of how Oedipus himself responds to and copes with the prophetic decla
ation concerning his life. As Knox puts it:

The meaning...is emphasized by Sophocles' presentation of the given situation, the action of the hero, and the nature of the catastrophe. The factor
common to all three is a prophecy, a prophecy given, apparently defied, and
finally vindicated. (p. 42)

It is this that provides the clue for understanding the play. Knox follows this clue

A5. In the play, Oedipus
(a) receives a prophecy;

This is vital for understanding the play. For, as Knox stresses, what Oedipus has done makes sense only in the context of the prophecy that spans Oedipus' life as a whole. It is what gives his parricide and incest meaning.

      A5. (continued) In the play, Oedipus
            (b) apparently defies a prophecy;

The play, as Knox views it, stresses Oedipus' defiance of prophecy. At the outset Oedipus appears to be a person who has "attempted to prove the oracle a liar" (p. 43), apparently successfully. In this Oedipus is attempting to undermine not just prophecy but the whole religious tradition and outlook. It is the truth of divinity that Oedipus challenges by his actions. The Chorus points out this aspect of the awesome significance of Oedipus' efforts: if the oracles fail in veracity, then religious observances and obedience go by the board (ll. 897-910).[9]

Oedipus directly attacks prophecy, and, thereby, traditional religion. For one thing, he mocks Tiresias, the representative of the god Apollo. Where were you when the Sphinx harassed the city, Oedipus taunts, and replies that it was by his wit that the city was saved. Jocasta, moreover, openly rejects prophecy as "worthless" and for this she has proof. With this Oedipus concurs (although, to be sure, he sends for the shepherd, just to confirm the details of her proof). Jocasta extends her point of view, rejecting divine order and sovereignty: "chance rules supreme" (ll. 977, 978). With this view Oedipus does not immediately concur but presses on with the inquiry. It is only at the very point that Jocasta discovers her error and ignorance that Oedipus comes around to the very position she herself has just abandoned, proclaiming himself "the child of Fortune" (l. 1080), thereby, too, denying divine order and rule.

      A5. (continued) In the play, Oedipus
            (c) learns eventually that prophecy cannot be so defied.

He learns that the very actions predicted of him have long since come true. Moreover,

      A6. Oedipus is like the person of Sophocles' own day who scoffs at
           religion, who favors arrogant humanism of the sort expressed for
           example in Protagoras' dictum that man is the measure of all
           things, and who needs to learn that such a view is ignorant and
           false. (pp. 44-47)

The play, says Knox, "takes a clear stand on one of the intellectual battlegrounds of the fifth century--the question of the truth or falsehood of prophecy" (pp. 43, 44). With Herodotus defending prophecy, and Thucydides, Euripides and Protagoras attacking it in one way or another, the issue was very much alive in Sophocles' own day. As Knox points out, the issue was a broad and vital one: "The question at issue in the debate

---

    [9]As Knox puts it (pp. 46, 47), the argument in the play runs as follows: (1) if the prophecy given to Laius does not correspond with reality, then prophecy is false. (2) But that prophecy does correspond with reality. Therefore prophecy is not false. This, however, is an invalid argument (fallacy of denying the antecedent). It is perhaps better to rephrase the first premise, if prophecy is false than the prophecy given to Laius does not correspond with reality, for this seems to make better sense and would lead validly to the desired conclusion.

was not just the truth or falsehood of prophecy, but the validity of the whole traditional religious view" (p. 46). The whole intellectual development in the play, with Oedipus' and Jocasta's mockery of prophecy to the affirmation of chance, with the tremendous emphasis on inquiry and one's own reason, stands as a symbolic representation of fifth-century Greek rationalism. It is a view, however, which according to Knox, Sophocles rejects.

As Knox construes it, the play is a demonstration of the futility of such humanistic rationalism. On the basis of A1 to A6, Knox concludes:

> ∴ The play is a terrifying affirmation of the truth of prophecy (and, consequently, of the whole traditional religious outlook). (p. 43)

Oedipus is presented by Sophocles as an "example" ($l.$ 1193)--an example to all of divine existence, sovereignty, and knowledge on the one hand, and of human ignorance and limitation on the other. Put more expansively, Knox claims:

> The play...is a reassertion of the religious view of a divinely ordered universe, a view which depends on the concept of divine omniscience, represented in the play by Apollo's prophecy. It is a statement which rejects the new concepts of the fifth-century philosophers and sophists, the new visions of a universe ordered by the laws of physics, the human intelligence, the law of the jungle, or the lawlessness of blind chance. (p. 47)

III

The play may be viewed in quite a different light than the interpretation give it by Knox. In this section I shall develop and defend another line of interpretation (it is essentially my own), one that stresses the role of inquiry in the play and which views Oedipus as a model inquirer. For ease of reference I shall refer to this line o interpretation as "argument B" and the main points as "B-claims."

Argument B goes as follows:

B1. In the play,
    (a) Oedipus persistently and relentlessly searches for the whole truth concerning the devastation that ravishes the city;

The play opens with a host of problems that require solution. For one thing, there is a commotion in front of an altar outside his palace, and Oedipus must deal with this. Then, more importantly, there is death and devastation throughout the city. Oedipus inquires, ponders, and acts.

The play thus begins by drawing our attention to two salient features of Oedipus' character: he is a rigorous inquirer and a decisive decision-maker. He sizes up and deals with situations in a resolute manner. He finds out what is wrong and then decides and acts. He finds out, for example, at first hand why the people are raising a commotion. He had, moreover, already taken steps to find a solution to Thebes' traum --even before the populace undertook processions to various religious shrines. The problem was already well under consideration.

Oedipus is presented not only as the inquirer but also as the suffering inquirer. Sophocles stresses this. Oedipus is heartbroken over the devastation of Thebes. Out of this suffering he seeks to find out what he can say or do--that is, to learn what is within his power to alter. This, indeed, is the very question he puts to the oracle. The oracle, however, does not answer this question but rather the more general question, namely, what must be done to alleviate the devastation.[10] In so doing it links the devastation to an unavenged murder.

The Prologue and the *parados* or opening choric recitative which immediately follows it present four different approaches to inquiry. The Chorus, for example, views the situation in theological terms: the situation is the result of Ares' activity, and the solution is to be found in calling for divine assistance (Athena, Artemis, Apollo, Dionysus) to save the city. The Chorus thus rejects inquiry.

The priest of Zeus, however, adopts a somewhat different stance. While calling upon Apollo to save the city, he also appeals to Oedipus to help, as being someone who had previously found a way to aid the city. He does not dismiss human help (as does the Chorus) but his approach to problem-solving is authoritarian in nature: seek the one who heroically, mysteriously, and single-handedly can deliver the city from affliction. Yet, like the Chorus, the priest of Zeus simply asks, *who* can save us? the difference being simply that in the latter instance, the "who" includes human as well as divine agency.

Creon, however, typifies a third approach to inquiry. He admits that it was a preoccupation with present concerns (the Sphinx) that had prevented a full-scale investigation into the cause of Laius' death. This approach represents aborted inquiry: it is not a rejection of inquiry *per se*, as in the previous two cases, but it does portray inquiry as shunted aside by lesser but more pressing concerns.

Oedipus alone represents resolute inquiry. He finds out what the situation is (it is the presence of an unknown assassin within the city, not the presence of Ares). He mulls over alternate solutions--indeed, he is the only one who is presented as thinking about the situation ("I...set my thoughts on countless paths, searching for an answer" (*l.* 67). He asks what is within his power to say or do that would alleviate the situation. He steadfastly determines to probe relentlessly for the unknown assassin. Oedipus is the inquirer: he does not claim to know. He knows he does not know and resolves, simply, to find a solution to the problem, as best he can.

B1. (continued) In the play
     (b) Oedipus patiently puts together the various pieces of the
         puzzle by reasoning out the connections and by demanding
         proof.

This characteristic, established at the outset in Oedipus' search for a way out of the Theban devastation, is reinforced in his rejection of Tiresias' edict. Tiresias' oracular pronouncement indicts Oedipus. But it is simply that: a claim without supporting evidence. Oedipus rejects this declaration. For one thing, he dismisses this unexpected--and unsubstantiated--answer as unprophetic and he attacks Tiresias' credentials. In addition, he questions the answer's rationality. After all, Oedipus himself, by his wit, had been able to solve the Sphinx's riddle when Tiresias could not. How, then, could Tiresias legitimately claim to know the truth? But, most importantly, the answer

---

[10]Perhaps there is a connection between this question and Oedipus' initial question, for the oracle, knowing Oedipus' character, might correctly assume that Oedipus, on hearing the answer to this question, would construe it as an answer to the question concerning what he should do to relieve the city's plight.

does not make sense unless--and here Oedipus' reasoning runs ahead of us--Tiresias and Creon are in conspiracy against him. What else could account, after all, for Tiresias' charge? In terms of what Tiresias has said, Oedipus' surmise is logical. Even the Chorus rejects Tiresias' claim, pointing out that while Zeus and Apollo may know, mortals do not, and citing Oedipus' success with the Sphinx.

Tiresias adamantly refuses to divulge the basis for his pronouncement, the very thing Oedipus demands. Without grounding, Tiresias' pronouncement is ineffectual and worthless. Indeed, while what Tiresias says is true, the truth is realized only as the result of a very different process. Truth is not perceived through divine utterance but by diligent, painstaking, all-too-human inquiry that takes many turns until the truth is brought to light by the interrogation of first-hand witnesses.

Rejection of the truth of Tiresias' claim does not mean, however, that Oedipus fails to take it seriously. He does, as the next scene in the play shows. In getting to the bottom of Tiresias' charge, Oedipus starts his inquiry off on the wrong track. He harangues Creon who admits he advised Oedipus to send for Tiresias, that he investigated the murder of Laius a long time ago, and that Tiresias had never then made any allegations against Oedipus. So, Oedipus concludes, if Tiresias had not acted under Creon's instructions, he would not have named Oedipus as Laius' assassin.

What seems here like a squabble--a "foolish war of words," as Jocasta puts it --is really a disclosure of the alacrity and astuteness of Oedipus' logical mind. He reasons (1) either Creon must be guilty of treachery or else he himself must be guilty (as Tiresias declared). He knows (2) he is not himself guilty. No evidence has been brought forward to counter this supposition. Thus it would follow, from (1) and (2), that Creon is at fault. The argument is valid. Indeed, as Oedipus points out the Chorus, if they fully understood what they were asking when they beseeched him to respect Creon's solemn oath and his past integrity, they are indirectly--and logically --accusing him of the guilt (*ll.* 655-659), for, according to Oedipus' first premise, the alternative to Creon's treachery is his own guilt. The Chorus recoils in confusion, but does not know how to exonerate both Creon and Oedipus.

The investigation then takes a different direction. Rather than advancing a conspiracy-hypothesis, Jocasta attempts to prove the powerlessness of divination and thus the baselessness of Tiresias' declaration. This unsettles Oedipus. He suspects the truth ("Am I cursed and cannot see it?" *ll.* 744, 745) but he is reluctant to admit it ("It cannot be--that the prophet sees" *l.* 747). He presses on with the investigation. He reasons that if the shepherd stated that robbers killed Laius, then he would be freed. As Jocasta points out, however, even if the shepherd changes his story and singles out an individual, Oedipus would still be exonerated, for Apollo had said Laius would be killed by his own son. With Oedipus pressing on with the investigation by sending for the shepherd, the Chorus piously praises the pure, immortal laws of Olympus and chides "seeking things unseasonable, unreasonable" (*l.* 875), thereby rejecting inquiry and advocating traditional religious obedience.

B1. (continued) In the play
(c) Oedipus eventually finds out the answer.

Gradually the pieces fall into place as Oedipus quizzes the Corinthian messenger and the shepherd, against all advice and in spite of their hesitation. Finally Oedipus knows--"I see it now" (*l.* 1182). He sees it only when the alternatives have been explored and when every piece has been testified to by eye-witnesses, that is, only when corroborated and grounded in personal veracity. The Chorus begins a lament

--men are nothing, wretched Oedipus, Time found him out, etc.--and here the Chorus is way off-target. It was not Time who found Oedipus out; it was, on the contrary, Oedipus who found out. The truth was the result of *his* active searching, not his passively having been sought out by Time. The Chorus completely misdescribes the situation here.

B1. (continued) In the play
    (d) Oedipus accepts the answer, no matter how painful and unex-
       pected the truth is.

Oedipus' first inclination is to blame fate (*l.* 1311) or Apollo (*l.* 1329), indeed, even the shepherd (*ll.* 1349,1350), but he soon rallies, emphasizing his role in blinding himself, in condemning himself, in doing what he had to do. He takes command of the situation, telling Creon to cast him out, arranging with Creon for Jocasta's funeral, and asking him to care for his daughters. He is very much the old Oedipus-- but with a difference: he now knows the truth and he has accepted it and its conse- quences.

The Chorus concludes with a farewell--"there goes Oedipus"--portraying him as a man who, once mighty and gifted, is now "drowning in waves of dread and despair" (*l.* 1527). Again the Chorus has misrepresented the situation: Oedipus, far from drowning, is thoroughly in charge of the situation. But notice: the Chorus is still unable to see what Oedipus has accomplished. They fail to see that it is the *same* Oedipus who was able to answer the Sphinx's riddle. The Chorus is blind to the Oedipus who searched, found out, and who has come to terms with the truth that *he*, by his wit, has uncovered.

B2. In this process, Oedipus has moved from the level of Appearance
    to the level of Reality; he has learned that man's life is in
    reality not free but fated; and he learns to live with this
    truth, in spite of its unpleasantness and unexpectedness.

Throughout the play there is an interesting contrast between Oedipus and the Chorus. The Chorus never advances in understanding. It never moves beyond a passive, unquestioning reliance on divine law and order. It calls upon a litany of gods/god- desses for help; it stresses obedience to the laws of heaven and disaster to those who defy these laws. It rejects inquiry; and it sees in Oedipus a man whom Time has found out. It articulates the whole posture of theological dependence.

This point of view has three consequences. For one thing, the Chorus is help- less: it cannot *do* anything to improve the situation in Thebes. Secondly, it cannot see the activity of Oedipus and the process *he* undergoes, as he passes from ignorance to knowledge through inquiry, thereby solving the problem that plagued the city. Fi- nally, it misunderstands the situation, for it cannot see, let alone value, the process whereby knowledge is accrued and truth disclosed. The Chorus learns, understands and sees nothing, and this is a consequence of its intellectual stance.

Oedipus, in contrast, grows in understanding. What seems at the outset to be a search for an unknown assassin becomes, in reality, a self-discovery of the truth about oneself. The problem, which at the outset appears to be *Thebes'* problem, is seen at the end to be *Oedipus'* problem. Oedipus has moved from the level of Appearance to the level of Reality. And he has done so through inquiry.

What Oedipus learns is that Reality is vastly different from Appearance--in- deed, his whole world has been turned upside-down, socially, personally, and intellec- tually. The truth is quite other than what appears initially to be the case. It is much more self-involving, less predictable, more surprising, than he had hitherto

thought. He also learns that, in spite of free, rational decisions, aided by acute
logic, he has already fulfilled in his life what was predicted of his actions.   In
Appearance, he is free; in Reality, he is fated.   This is not to say that there is
a contradiction here between freedom and fate, any more than there is one between
not-knowing and knowing.   Rather Oedipus' knowledge at the end is torn from the de-
ceptions and falsehoods of Appearance and elevated to the apprehension of the truth
of Reality.   The truth is painful, burdensome, and alienating, and Oedipus must ada
We see him at the end, beginning this adaptation, leaving others behind.

> B3.   Oedipus, then, is like the humanist seeker after truth of Sopho-
> cles' own time, the one who relentlessly pushes inquiry beyond
> customarily accepted opinions to the truth beyond, no matter what
> the personal cost, and who accepts this truth, no matter how un-
> palatable or how unpredictable.

Ever since the days of Heraclitus and Parmenides, it had been known (1) tha
there is a gap between Appearance and Reality, and (2) that Reality is quite unlike
Appearance.   The natural philosophers before Heraclitus and Parmenides, and especially the Pythagoreans, had encountered this, for both the principle of unity and th
principle of differentiation were quite unlike anything met by the senses.   Parmeni
in particular drove the wedge deeply between the two: the Way of Opinion, the way
change and of opposites, which cannot be thought, and is not, on the one hand; and
Way of Truth, the way of the changelessly eternal, on the other.   What is is vastly
different from what is commonly (and erroneously) supposed to be: Reality is "unbe
gotten...imperishable...whole...immovable...complete...since it is now, all at once
one and continuous."[11]

Sophocles, too, exploits the difference between Appearance and Reality and
shows us a person in movement, one who successfully makes the transition into Reali
In so doing, Sophocles contributes at least three very significant points to the on
going discussion.

For one thing, he portrays the power of inquiry, for it is the means by whi
Appearance is transcended.   The Chorus, for example, never attains this state but r
mains locked into the illusions and distortions of Appearance.   And while Tiresias
have apprehended the Truth directly and Jocasta may have intuited it indirectly, in
neither case is true opinion grounded in knowledge.[12]   Only Oedipus, the rational i
quirer, achieves this.

For another thing, knowledge of nature is depicted by Sophocles as involvin
knowledge of the self: the two are not disassociated.   In inquiring into the woes
Thebes--devastation in the natural and social world--Oedipus is driven back to what
is personal.   The forces that control the natural and social order are also the for
that control the self.   Nature, society, and self are each equally part of destiny t
works itself out.   Inquiry into nature and knowledge of nature cannot therefore be
truth about nature: it is intrinsically truth about the human self.

---

[11]Parmenides, *Way of Truth*.   Selection 6.10 in John Manley Robinson, *An Intr
duction to Early Greek Philosophy* (Boston: Houghton Mifflin 1968) 113.

[12]Cf. the discussion between Socrates and Meno, *Meno* 97a-99a; cf. also the
discussion between Awida and Bardaisan in *The Book of the Laws of the Countries*,
trans. H. J. W. Drijvers (Assen: Van Gorcum 1965) 7-9.

Finally, the passage from Appearance into Reality exacts a tremendous price: deep personal pain and anguish, the sort of horrible suffering Oedipus undergoes so acutely. It is true that his inquiry is launched in suffering, but it ends in a suffering of a much greater intensity. *Oedipus Tyrannus* is pre-eminently a play that demonstrates the profound personal cost of inquiry.

In many ways, Sophocles' play anticipates the message of the Cave Allegory in Plato's *Republic*.[13] Both stress the move from Appearance to Reality, the crucial role of inquiry, the otherness and unfamiliarity of Reality, the alienation and solitariness the rational pursuit of Reality entails, and the high personal pain of such a pursuit. Both make the same epistemological point and both do so dramatically.

Oedipus, then, is like the seeker after truth in Sophocles' own time. He is the one who trusts in reason, logic, and inquiry to open up and uncover the truth that lies hidden, one who takes clues from but who is not bound by the dictates of religious insight. Such an inquirer is not only persistent, relentless, and courageous; he is also a sufferer, alienated, and lonely, for that is the personal cost of seeking Truth.

On this line of interpretation, claims B1 - B3, the following conclusion is reached about the meaning of the play:

∴ *Oedipus Tyrannus* is a story about the dreadful agony of human inquiry and the horrible price paid for growth in knowledge and true understanding.

As is readily evident, argument B differs considerably from argument A.

There are, of course, other quite different interpretations of *Oedipus Tyrannus*. Omitting the discussion such a view would obviously require, one timely but somewhat facetious interpretation goes as follows (let us refer to this as "argument C"):

C1. Both Oedipus and Jocasta seek to outwit a prophecy.

C2. In the course of the play, both Oedipus and Jocasta
(a) discover that they have not succeeded in outwitting the prophecy, and
(b) respond in their own way to this discovery.

C3. Oedipus discovers the truth by dint of slow patient reasoning; Jocasta, by a quick, perceptive, intuitive realization.

∴ The play shows the superiority of intuitive reasoning over methodical deduction.

This argument, focussing more than traditional views of the play do on Jocasta and the process she undergoes, produces quite a different interpretative thrust from arguments A and B.

In addition, Philip Vellacott has recently offered a new interpretation of *Oedipus Tyrannus*, one that develops an interesting and challenging interpretative al-

[13]*Republic* 514A-521B.

ternative to Knox's position and what Vellacott calls the traditional view.[14] Accor
ing to Vellacott, the traditional view holds that Oedipus is ignorant of his true id
tity, at least up to $l.$ 716 ("at a junction of three highways"). He disputes this
view. Without doing justice to the richness of his discussion on behalf of each ma
point, his argument can be briefly sketched as follows (let us refer to this as "arc
ment D"):

D1. There are six questions which (in Vellacott's judgment) have never
     been properly answered.(see pp. 114ff)

D2. These questions can be accommodated if we suppose
     (a) that on the surface the play presents Oedipus as ignorant of
         his true identity, and yet
     (b) that "beneath the surface" the play shows "with complete
         clarity" that "Oedipus knew as soon as he had entered Thebes
         who it was he had killed, and was aware of his parricide and
         incest from the first night of his marriage." (p. 129)

D3. There is evidence for D2(b).

∴. "Sophocles intended the *careful reader* (and perhaps some unusually
    acute spectators) to see Oedipus as having been aware of his true
    relationship to Laius and Jocasta ever since the time of his mar-
    riage." (p. 104)

The support for premise D3, a crucial one, is provided by a detailed study of each
portion of the play (see pp. 125-246) and comes from clues provided in Oedipus' discussions with Tiresias, Creon and Jocasta (e.g., in Oedipus' "flying off the handle"
at Tiresias and Creon); in what Oedipus, Creon and the Chorus do not say (e.g., in
not suggesting that the "one man who ran away" from the murder of Laius--$l.$118--be
summoned immediately and interrogated); and in what the careful reader can be pre-
sumed to have figured out concerning what Oedipus would undoubtedly have realized
upon entering Thebes and marrying Jocasta. The play thus becomes, on this line of
interpretation, a study of the terror of admitting to oneself and to others the trut
about oneself, a truth one in a sense knows, and yet, because of a carefully culti-
vated façade, one knows not.

IV

In the preceding two sections, a particular interpretative controversy has be
examined. Four different interpretative positions on Sophocles' *Oedipus Tyrannus* ha
been sketched, two of them (A and B) in some critical detail. We started out by ask
in all naivete, what does Sophocles' *Oedipus Tyrannus* mean? In reply, we were greet
with a great variety of answers. Arguments A, B, C, and D present four quite differ
views concerning what the play means, as their respective conclusions clearly indica
I take this situation of interpretative diversity to be typical of interpretive cont
versies generally. Put schematically, the typical answer to the question (call it
"question I"):

---

[14]Philip Vellacott, *op. cit.* References to this work in Argument D are plac
in parentheses following the quoted or referred to material.

(I) What does text t mean?

is of the form:

(i) Text t means interpretation i_1, interpretation i_2, ..., interpretation i_n.

(or, to put it more tersely, t means $i_1, i_2, ..., i_n$).

An answer to this sort of question (I) may be found to be overwhelming. Indeed, an answer of form (i) is very difficult to construe. For instance, in asking
question (I), we may have initially expected in reply an answer of quite another sort,
one having the following form:

(ii) t means i_x.

or, at worst, some slight divergence in meanings. Yet the conclusions to interpretative arguments A, B, C, and D differ markedly as to the play's meaning. They for-
bid any answer to (I) along the lines indicated by form (ii). We are confronted,
then, with having to make sense of an answer of form (i) to question (I).

The situation whereby an answer of form (i) is regarded as the answer to question (I) may be variously construed. Some may argue that an answer of form (i) is all
one can expect to question (I), plays, persons, and interpretations being what they
are. On this approach one would simply have to reform one's expectations to correspond
to the alleged exigencies of the interpretative situation.

Even so, on this approach, one would still be left with the question how (i)
is an informative answer to question (I), let alone whether it is an answer to (I) at
all. Others would contend, moreover, that there is something wrong with an answer of
form (i), namely that it is not an answer to the question asked. It is simply unresponsive, this approach contends, to answer the question, "*what* does text t mean?"
with a catalog or series of meanings. An "answer" of form (i) represents, on this
view, an inability or a refusal to answer the question posed. Shortly (in section V
of this paper) I shall argue that this latter view, somewhat modified, is correct, for
an interesting reason not yet apparent.

There is another puzzling aspect of an answer of form (i) which may be expressed formally as follows: how are the commas in the answer to be interpreted, as
"and" or as "or"? If the former, then an answer of form (i) would read that a text t
means intrepretation i_1 *and* interpretation i_2 *and* so on. Are we therefore to accept
the view that the text means each and every interpretation it is given? This would
appear to be a position congruent with the view that an answer of form (i) is all one
can expect to question (I). If, on the other hand, the commas in (i) are construed
as "or" (in its exclusive sense), then the answer is viewed as setting forth a variety of alternative meanings for the text. This immediately raises the specter of
selection, for to say of a text t that it means interpretation i_x *or* (exclusive sense)
interpretation i_y *or* (exclusive sense) interpretation i_z is either to say that some
interpretation or interpretations are to be accepted and others not, or to say that
none of these interpretations are to be accepted, but not to say that all interpretations are to be accepted. When viewed along these lines, interpretative diversity
raises at least two important problems concerning selectivity. For one thing, in terms
of what criteria are interpretations to be selected? For another, what are they to be
selected as (e.g., as correct interpretations, plausible interpretations, etc.)? Con-
struing the commas in (i) as "or" is, in a sense, already to take a significant step

towards an answer to question (I) of form (ii), for it introduces into an understanding of interpretations a radical dissimilarity: it implies that not all interpretations are to be viewed as equally acceptable.

There is yet a further difficulty with an answer of form (i). The situation of interpretative diversity is by no means rare, where, for one reason or another, the one and the same text is given differing interpretations by their interpreters.[1] Scholarship in the humanities is familiar with this facet of research. Such diversity, however, raises profound meta-interpretative problems concerning what constitutes textual meaning, how this can be discerned, and whether or not the search for one and only one interpretation of a text is even legitimate, let alone feasible. Historicity, the kinds of questions the interpreter asks of a text, the tradition within which the interpreter stands, intentional textual ambiguity, etc., have all been cited as diversity-producing factors.

The meta-interpretative situation before us now, however, is of a different sort: not only is there diversity in meaning, there is interpretative conflict. The conclusions of two of the interpretative arguments are incompatible, two interpretations being incompatible when both cannot be true.[16] The conclusion of argument B is for example, completely at odds with the conclusion of argument A. For A, the play represents an affirmation of the traditional religious outlook; for B, on the other hand, it is an exemplification of the valor and cost of inquiry. It cannot be the case that both are correct, and one cannot therefore accept both conclusions. Similarly, the conclusion of argument D stands opposed to any view of Oedipus which would make him out to be truly ignorant of his true identity at the outset of the play (as both premise A5 and premise B1 would appear to indicate).

The incompatibility goes even farther, as a comparison of arguments A and B would indicate. It does not lie in premises A1, A2, A3 or A4 which, on the whole, in

---

[15] Note, for instance, the interpretative controversy concerning the meaning of Shakespeare's *Hamlet*: Morris Weitz, *Hamlet and the Philosophy of Literary Criticism* (Chicago: University of Chicago Press 1964); Paul Gottschalk, *The Meanings of Hamlet* (Albuquerque: University of New Mexico Press 1972). Consider also the interpretative controversy concerning the interpretation of the parables of Jesus: see for instance, Dan Otta Via, Jr., *The Parables* (Philadelphia: Fortress 1967); John Dominic Crossan, *In Parables* (New York: Harper & Row 1973); Norman Perrin, *Jesus and the Language of the Kingdom* (Philadelphia: Fortress 1976); etc.

[16] The topic of incompatible interpretations of a work has received some attention in a number of works, although it has not always been made clear under what circumstances one interpretation is said to be "incompatible" with another. See, for instance, the following studies which touch, at least in part, on the topic of incompatible interpretations: Joseph Margolis, "The Logic of Interpretation," in Margolis, *The Language of Art and Art Criticism* (Detroit: Wayne State University Press 1965); Monroe C. Beardsley, *The Possibility of Criticism* (Detroit: Wayne State University Press 1970); Denis Dutton, "Plausibility and Aesthetic Interpretation," *Canadian Journal of Philosophy* 7 (1977) 327-340; Joseph Margolis, "Robust Relativism" in Margolis (ed.), *Philosophy Looks at the Arts* (Philadelphia: Temple University Press 1978); and John Reichert, *Making Sense of Literature* (Chicago: University of Chicago Press 1978). See also Jack W. Meiland, "Interpretation as a Cognitive Discipline," *Philosophy and Literature* 2 (1978) 23-45, which discusses multiple interpretations of the same text.

no way conflict with the central points in argument B (although "catastrophe" in A4, unless a technical term, might be construed by B as too strong a word). Clearly premises A6 and B3 are at odds, for each see Oedipus as being like a different sort of person in Sophocles' own day. Why this is so rests on a further point of incompatibility: B1 and B2 are incompatible with A5. Both set out a different understanding of what Oedipus himself undergoes in the play.

The situation of interpretative incompatibility poses yet another problem for understanding an answer of form (i) to question (I). Are we therefore to understand by an answer of this sort that all interpretations, even incompatible ones, are to be accepted? This view would be congruent with the position that regards an answer of form (i) as all one can expect to question (I). It is also congruent with the view that regards the commas in (i) as "and." It is a view, however, that poses considerable problems of its own concerning what could be meant by "incompatibility" in such a context and how two or more "incompatible" interpretations could be simultaneously entertained by any one truth-regarding and truth-abiding individual. On the other hand, perhaps an answer of form (i) to question (I) should be regarded as again implying a principle of selectivity, whereby one of the incompatible interpretations would be selected (and the others rejected), or else all rejected, but not where all such incompatible interpretations would be accepted.

An answer of form (i) to question (I) raises, then, some intricate puzzles. Three important ones have been cited: (1) how (i) is to be construed *as an answer* to question (I); (2) how the commas in (i) are to be construed; and (3) how the situation is to be understood whereby one interpretation (say i_x) is incompatible with another interpretation (say i_y) of the same text. If we stay simply on the level of interpretation we shall be stymied in our attempts to unravel these matters. We must move, then, to a meta-interpretative level so as to reflect on and hopefully understand better the interpretative situation before us. We have a text; we have several quite different, even incompatible, interpretations offered of it. What are we to make of this situation? I shall call this question "question (II)." Put more formally, (II) is as follows:

> (II) What are we to make of the situation whereby the question, "what does text t mean?" receives as an answer a reply of the following form: "text t means interpretation i_1, interpretation i_2, ..., interpretation i_n"?

Question (II) is an important, primary meta-interpretative question. In what follows I shall explore a few aspects of interpretative controversy that shed some light on unravelling the complex nature of question (II).

V

It is important to note that we have come to question (II) out of an interpretative controversy in which the meaning of a text is disputed. This disputative aspect of textual interpretation is significant, and much overlooked. In a sense, an answer of form (i) to question (I) is apt to mislead us into thinking that we simply have a text and a series of alternative interpretations. While important, this is only one part of the contentious nature of textual interpretation. The matter is much more complex. It is not that interpreter$_1$ says "t means i_1"; interpreter$_2$ says "t means i_2"; and so on, as a series of alternative edicts or pronouncements upon the text's meaning. This understanding of the situation would ignore a substantial element in the disputative character of textual interpretation.

An interpreter does not just focus on a text; he attends also to other interpretations of the same text. In so doing, he develops and presents his own interpretation in the context of other understandings of the same text. He does not simply say, "t means i_x." Rather the situation should be visualized schematically more along these lines:

> interpreter$_1$ says "t means i_1"; interpreter$_2$, on the other hand, says, "No, it does not; t means i_2."

The "No, it does not" part is significant, for it serves to indicate an additional dimension of the controversial, contentious, and argumentative nature of textual interpretation.

Knox, for example, in working out what we have called "argument A," rejects Aristotle's view of the play (see premise A4) as well as all interpretative positions that regard the play as a tragedy of fate (see A1). Argument B rejects Knox's view of the process Oedipus undergoes in the play (see B3). Argument D rejects the position presupposed in arguments A (see A5) and B (see B1) that Oedipus is not aware of his real identity at the play's beginning (see D2). Argument C, moreover, stands opposed to all interpretations (such as arguments A, B, and D) which focus exclusively on what Oedipus undergoes in the play to the total neglect of Jocasta. More could have been made out of this aspect of interpretation in our reconstruction of arguments A, B, C, and D, to show not only how interpretative positions are presented but also how they are advanced *against* other rival candidates in the field. In presenting a major interpretative argument there are usually a host of associated, subsidiary arguments. Enough has been said, however, to show that interpretation is worked out, not just by examining the text, but also by glancing sideways at the results of other interpretative efforts.

Textual interpretation is controversial, then, not just because a text has a series of different interpretations but also because these interpretations compete with one another. This aspect of textual interpretation presents some interesting features.

Five Models of Interpretation

For one thing, the controversial nature of interpretation indicates certain basic structural features with which the study of interpretation should be concerned. These can be described in a series of models--models which serve to focus on the main structural elements of textual interpretation and which are useful in indicating the theoretical concerns raised by each sort of model.[17]

Frequently textual interpretation has been treated simply as a triadic relationship. This can be variously put, depending on what one thinks an interpreter does with a text when interpreting it. On one version,

(1) an interpreter provides (2) an interpretation of (3) a text.

---

[17]For my use of "model," see Max Black, *Models and Metaphors* (Ithaca: Cornell University Press 1962); Mary B. Hesse, *Models and Analogies in Science* (London: Sheed and Ward 1963); and Ian T. Ramsey, *Models and Mystery* (London: Oxford University Press 1964).

He interprets *it* so as to come up with a statement of *its meaning*.[18] On another version,

      (1) an interpreter gives (2) an interpretation to (3) a text.[19]

The second formulation, while more colloquial, seems to close, or at least to limit, the possibility of reciprocity when interpreter meets text.

However the triadic model be phrased, it provides a framework for discussing textual interpretation. It also sets attention on some particular meta-interpretative matters:

    (1) how the three elements in the relationship function, separately and in interaction;

    (2) what the interpreter must take into account when providing/giving an interpretation of/to a text;

    (3) how the "providing of an interpretation" relates to the "giving of an interpretation to" a text;

    (4) the characteristics of the interpreter that impinge on textual interpretation (e.g., historicity, presuppositions, "horizon", etc.);

    (5) characteristics of the text that impinge on interpretation (e.g., its general linguistic character, authorship, its edited nature [if applicable], its provenance, etc.);

    (6) how the third element (i.e. texts) relates (if at all) to other items which interpreters are said to interpret (e.g., works of art, events, persons, etc.);

and so on. What is often overlooked in these discussions, however, is the relationship of element (2) to element (3), i.e., of interpretation to text. What criteria must what is said about a text satisfy in order to count as an interpretation of that text? After all, not everything that can be said about a text constitutes an interpretation of that text.

---

[18]Cf. Beardsley, *op. cit.*, who describes (literary) interpretation in the following way: "...any such statement, or set of statements, used to report discovered meaning in a literary text I shall call a 'literary interpretation'" (p. 38). In an earlier work, Beardsley had described interpretation as verbally unfolding or disclosing meaning. See his "The Limits of Critical Interpretation," in Sidney Hook (ed.), *Art and Philosophy* (New York: New York University Press 1966) 61-87. This view is strongly criticized by Joseph Margolis, "Three Problems in Aesthetics," in Sidney Hook, *op. cit.*, 262-270.

[19]Cf. Margolis' distinction between describing and interpreting. The latter suggests "...a touch of virtuosity, an element of performance, a shift from a stable object whose properties, however complex, are simply enumerable to an object whose properties pose something of a puzzle or a challenge--with emphasis on the solution of the puzzle, or on some inventive use of the materials present, on the added contribution of the interpreter, and on a certain openness toward possible alternative interpretations." See "Describing and Interpreting Works of Art," in Margolis, *The Language of Art and Art Criticism* chap. 5.

20

Certainly these three elements, their nature and their various interrelationships, are essential to any understanding of textual interpretation. The questions
this model poses remain fundamental for all additional models, although the matter
grows increasingly more intricate as additional elements are added.

Some have added to the complexity by adding a fourth element. Bultmann (and
others) have added the "for whom" an interpretation is provided, the logical model
here being tetradic in kind:

(1) an interpreter provides (2) an interpretation of (3) a text for
(4) someone.

(Call this "someone" the "interpretation-recipient.") On this model, then, the interpreter is seen as a kind of mediator, one who stands between the text and the interpretation-recipient so as to present its meaning (with all its vitality and impact) to
him (in terms he can comprehend). The process of demythologizing is one proposal
for accomplishing the task of interpretative mediation for at least one sort of text.[20]

As is readily evident, a tetradic model opens up a new series of questions,
as the interrelationships between the four elements are examined. The exigencies of
the designated interpretation-recipients, and the interpreter's understanding of them,
seem to play a role in what the interpreter has to do to/with a text so as to present
its meaning to them. Indeed *its* meaning becomes enormously complicated, for, on this
model, the meaning is not simply *its* meaning, nor even *its* meaning as interpreted by
the interpreter (in terms he can grasp), but rather *its* meaning as interpreted by the
interpreter in terms he thinks the interpretation-recipient can grasp. The transformations proposed here are immensely complex.

Another quite different tretradic model arises out of an appreciation of the
"by whom" texts are written, thus adding the author as a fourth element:

(1) an interpreter provides (2) an interpretation of (3) a text which
(4) an author has composed.

Both Dilthey and Hirsch have stressed this fourth element, although in quite different ways. This model again focusses inquiry in a specific direction, as the interrelationships between the author and the other three elements are explored. Questions
arise concerning the necessity, desirability, and possibility of affinities between
interpreter and author, and the bearing this may have on the understanding of the
text. Questions arise, moreover, concerning the role of the author's intended meaning, access to it, and its relevance to the interpretation of the text. Other questions concern the absence of the fourth element in any perspicuous way for many sorts
of texts, notably many myths, epics and sagas whose authorship cannot now be indicated

Both tetradic models could conceivably be combined into a pentadic model, in-
corporating both the "for whom" and the "by whom" a text is written. I will not pur-

---

[20]Allegorical hermeneutics--for example, of the sort proposed by Origen, John
Cassian, or Augustine--represents another way of accomplishing interpretative mediation. On this approach, the interpreter relates the text's meaning to a variety of
interpretative levels, depending on the interpretation-recipient's level of comprehen-
sion. The interpreter, moreover, on this approach also bears in mind when interpreting
certain texts (e.g., the Old Testament) the new reality in which the interpretation-
recipient lives (i.e., on the post-resurrection side of Jesus' life).

sue this fourth model here but will turn instead to another sort of model in some greater detail.

Both the triadic and the two tetradic models mentioned ignore an important dimension of the interpretation of texts, namely its highly controversial aspect. Interpreters do not just provide interpretations of texts, whether additionally for someone or in explicit recognition of the author by whom it came into being. They do so usually in the context of other interpreters having interpreted the same text and having done so differently, differently, that is, from each other and differently from the one the interpreter himself is about to provide. As has already been mentioned, interpreters interpret, not only in interaction with the text, but in full cognizance of other interpreters and interpretations of the same text. This points to a pentadic model of textual interpretation:

(1) an interpreter provides (2) an interpretation of (3) a text in the context of (4) of other interpreters who have provided (5) their interpretations of the same text.

As this pentadic model indicates, interpretations are not just provided. They are presented in the context of contentiousness in which they have to vie for existence with other different conflicting interpretative positions regarding the same text. In a word, they must fend for themselves in a hostile environment.

The triadic model, even augmented by author or interpretation-recipients, or both, represents a too restrictive, too private, even perhaps too friendly a view of textual interpretation. Interpretation is strife-ridden. The particular interpretative controversy we examined exemplified this; it is a situation which represents the usual circumstance in which the scholarly interpretation of texts, be they literary, legal, philosophical, religious, historical, etc., proceeds.

Each model has hitherto served to shift the focus of inquiry in a specific direction. The same is true of this pentadic model as the five elements are viewed in their various interrelationships. A number of questions emerge. For one thing, how are the relationships between the various interpretations of the same text to be understood? Where, how, and why do they differ? And of what significance are their differences? For another thing, how does the interpretation the interpreter is proposing relate to prior interpretations? How does it get "established"? Moreover, how do all these competing interpretations relate to the text of which they are (putatively) interpretations? Are they all equally "interpretations of the text"? Are they to be spoken of in terms of correctness, or ranked according to some scale and conception of merit, or viewed as "plausible", or deemed acceptable as interpretations as "interesting" or "challenging" or "perceptive" comments on the text, etc.?

In other words, on this model, the questions that are thrust into prominence are ones that concern how interpretations relate to each other and to the text. Ultimately this model throws open the more radical questions--what is a text, if it be such as to permit so many divergent interpretations of itself? Indeed, what is it to be an interpretation of a text? In what relation must *it* stand to the text?

This pentadic model, one suggested by and congruent with the controversial nature of interpretation, has received scant attention.

Interpretative Reasons

In addition to the pentadic structure of interpretation, there is another me interpretative aspect that arises from an explicit acknowledgement of the disputati character of interpretation. It should be apparent that the answer to question (I) considerably more complex than the answer of form (i) would indicate. The answer gi to question (I) is not just that the text means this or that interpretation. Rather the answer takes the form that the text means such-and-such *for such-and-such reason* This is readily evident from the interpretative controversy we examined: in each ca the interpreters in arguments A, B, C, and D backed up their interpretative position with reasons. Put schematically, the answer to question (I) takes the following for

(iii) text t means interpretation i_x because... (and here a variety
of reasons are cited).

In other words, interpretations are not simply given. They are justified, defended, and argued for. Interpretative positions come equipped with interpretative reasons.

Interpreting, then, in the context of controversy, has the following specifi structure: an interpretative position supported by a variety of interpretative rea sons. The structure is important, for it indicates a direction. However interpreta tions are *discovered* (and here, surely, many factors play a prominent role: creativ ity, insight, scholarly abilities, etc.), when they are offered on the public stage as interpretations, they are presented with the full understanding that they need to be established or *justified*. It is recognized that an interpretation will be inspec not only in relation to the text of which it is an interpretation, but also in relat to other interpretations of the same text of which it is a rival. As a result, inte pretations can never be edicts or proclamations of a text's meaning. Because of wha an interpretation must do--express the text's meaning in an arena in which other com peting interpretative efforts aim to do precisely that--it has quite a different cha acter.

Interpretative Arguments

In recognizing that interpretative positions come equipped with interpretati reasons, we have thereby acknowledged that interpretations are presented in the form of interpretative arguments. This is the form of interpretation--not edicts, pronou ments, proclamations, or any other form of sheer assertiveness that such-and-such is the case. Interpretations exhibit all the common features of arguments: conclusion (i.e., the interpretative position), premises (i.e., the interpretative reasons), an support for the individual premises--indeed, the whole panoply of "main arguments" a "mini-arguments" which make up the fabric of disputation.[21] This is a significant a pect of interpretation, one that has been overlooked, although it has always been be fore us, in interpretative practice. Argument is the mode of interpretation.

Recognition of this form is important to meta-interpretative inquiry. For or thing, it is instrumental in value. It helps to pinpoint key claims, to organize su porting considerations, to show on what grounds an interpretative position is advance to indicate how an interpretative position is defended, and so on. Good interpretat

---

[21]See the author's *Anatomy of Argument* (forthcoming, Fall 1980).

practice has always reflected this. It has, in addition, significant theoretical import.

Recognition of the argumentative form of textual interpretation enables us, moreover, to differentiate between the *interpretative result* (i.e., the conclusion of the interpretative argument) and the *interpretative reasons* (i.e., the premises of the interpretative argument). This distinction is important, for the claim that many texts are such that they are capable of receiving diverse, differing, or conflicting interpretations is imprecise. *Wherein* they differ is crucial. Interpretations that differ do differ not only in interpretative result but also in interpretative reasons. This approach, therefore, has the advantage of readily locating wherein disputes lie.

Thirdly, recognition of the argumentative form of textual interpretation also makes clear the basis on which differing interpretative results differ--i.e., in the premises which constitute their respective lines of reasoning. In examining interpretative disputes from a meta-interpretative perspective, this has the thrust of transferring hermeneutic attention away from the obvious discrepancy (two or more diverse or conflicting interpretative conclusions) to what is more subtle and complex (the divergent interpretative reasons). By these means, points of agreement and disagreement can be readily singled out, as was done, for instance, in section IV of this paper for arguments A, B, C, and D. This shift to differing interpretative reasons constitutes an important step in the meta-interpretative investigation of interpretative disputes.

Fourthly, once the meta-interpretative focus has shifted to the reasons for an interpretative conclusion, then the matter becomes one of judging which interpretative premises are well or better defended by supporting considerations. It puts the onus on the interpreters to defend their interpretative reasons and to challenge the differing interpretative reasons of others--*by the evidence*. The hermeneutic shift, then, is not simply to the interpretative premises as such but to the supporting considerations that underlie each premise that plays an important role in the interpretative dispute in question. In the dispute concerning arguments A and B on the meaning of *Oedipus Tyrannus*, for instance, meta-interpretative focus should properly be placed on the reasons that support A5 on the one hand versus the reasons that support B1 and B2 on the other, for *that* is what is at issue.

In essence this approach has the enormous theoretical import of taking meta-interpretative emphasis away from the persons involved--the focus on the author and the interpreter so prevalent in various forms of hermeneutics of the post-Schleiermacher period--and placing it upon the relationship between what is said about a text by way of interpreting it and the text itself. This relationship, the one between the interpretation (i.e., interpretative conclusion and interpretative premises) and the text itself, is what should bear the brunt of meta-interpretative scrutiny. This places hermeneutics directly in the same sort of square of controversy in which other kinds of disputes--e.g., legal, academic, scientific, moral, governmental, etc.-- find expression, challenge,and perhaps eventual resolution.

This makes explicit that interpretations are texts written about texts. What is being compared are the contents of scraps of paper: the text, an interpretation, other interpretations of the same text. The thrust of this approach--indeed, that of the whole pentadic model of textual interpretation--is simply to make central in meta-interpretative inquiry how these elements relate. How must the interpreting

writing relate to the interpreted text so that the former constitutes an interpreta
tion of the latter? And how do two or more interpreting writings relate to one another? These two questions now become the pivotal ones in meta-interpretation.

This is not the place to work out a full-scale study of interpretative argu
ments. A study of this sort would systematically examine some representative kinds
of interpretative arguments, culled from a detailed analysis of good interpretative
practice. It would note how interpretations are advanced, how they are defended, he
and wherein interpretations of the same text differ, what kinds of evidence are int
duced in establishing an interpretative conclusion, what kinds of evidence are reje
or modified in the course of an interpretative controversy, how other interpretatio
are argued against, and so forth. The study would focus on the sorts of evidence i
terpretative arguments typically cite.

Such a study is clearly well beyond the perimeters of this paper. It is im
portant, however, to see that such a study is the meta-interpretative direction tha
attention to the features of interpretative controversy places before us. Nor is t
the appropriate place to work out a "logic" of textual interpretation,[22] although,
submit, it is in this direction that such a logic is to be found. A logic of textua
interpretation would be a logic of interpretative arguments. Nor is this the place
work out a hermeneutics of fidelity. I suggest, however, that it is in this directi
that such a hermeneutics is to be found, in working out and assessing the interpreta
tion that is best supported by the text, i.e., in ascertaining the best interpretati
argument for that text.

This meta-interpretative approach raises some important problems, however.
For example, for one thing, how should the relationship between interpretation and
text be characterized? This question needs answering so as to enable us to distinguish between comments made about a text that constitute genuine interpretations of
that text from those comments that fail to be. For another, when ought an interpretative claim (either conclusion or premise) be said to be "well supported" or "ade-
quately defended" by a text? The relation of textual interpretation to its textual
evidential base needs to be made clear if the notion of "being faithful to" the text
is to have precise meaning. And, thirdly, what kinds of evidence are evidence for
the truth of interpretative claims? Should we admit, for example, as a fundamental
meta-interpretative principle, the position that

> unless there is good reason to the contrary, the primary evidence
> for the truth of an interpretative claim is textual evidence?

Such a meta-interpretative "rule of evidence" would rule out as evidence for an inte
pretation such considerations as information about the author, about extra-textual
contexts (such as, of its first having been written, of its transmission, of its being read today), and of the interpreter, etc., unless good reasons are cited by the
interpreter for admitting such evidence into the discussion.

Citing these important problems is not to admit defeat. Rather it is to sug
gest, on the basis of the meta-interpretative approach advocated here, the proper lo

---

[22]This direction differs considerably from that suggested by Margolis in "Th
Logic of Interpretation," and from that indicated by Richard Shusterman, "The Logic
of Interpretation," *Philosophical Quarterly* 28 (1978) 310-324.

cation of hermeneutic inquiry. It is also to point out that in this inquiry, meta-interpretation is not alone. The relation of claim to evidence is a central problem in any area of endeavor in which disputes are investigated by argument.

... *Means* ...: *Some qualifications*

Interpretative arguments seek to establish what a text means. This involves argumentation on two fronts. First of all, in relation to the text itself, it involves an argument whose conclusion is of the following form:

$\therefore$ t means i_x.

Secondly, in relation to other interpretations of the same text, the interpretation has to establish itself as an interpretation--to look after its own credentials, as it were. This involves an associated argument (or arguments) whose conclusion(s) is of the following form:

$\therefore$ t does not mean i_y, i_z, etc. (where i_y, i_z, etc. have been advanced as interpretations of the text by other interpreters).

Interpretative arguments, then, argue both what a text means and (at least with respect to some other interpretations offered of the same text) what it does not mean. This was evident in our presentation of arguments A, B, C, and D in sections II and III above and in the analysis of their various points of disagreement in section IV.

Interpretative arguments provide the way in which question (I) is answered. How they answer question (I), however, is important, for they indicate a basic lack of clarity about the question itself that needs now to be noted. The "means" in question (I), and in the answer to question (I), needs to be qualified in certain ways. One way of accomplishing this is as follows.

In reading the Book of Job, for instance, an interpreter might hazard the interesting interpretative guess that contrary to one usual line of interpretation that regards the work as about Job and his suffering, the work is really about God and the Covenant, a work that really probes two main issues: (1) whether life lived within the Covenantal relationship is really a blessed life, and (2) whether there is any assurance that God himself is honoring the Covenant. Seen in this light, the Book of Job would represent a refreshing reappraisal of, perhaps even a sharp corrective to, prophetic edicts on these matters. This interpreter has not yet worked out the details of this line of interpretation--i.e., he has not yet formulated an interpretative argument. He has simply indicated his impression of what the work *might* mean.

In this case, the work *might* mean this, although, of course, it *might* not. We would have to wait and see, to await, in other words, the formulation and presentation of an interpretative argument on behalf of the interpretative position being advanced, and judge it by the evidence it presents in its defense. As it stands, the view simply represents one possibility, one interesting interpretative avenue to explore. There is nothing very definite, nothing very settled, about this interpretative hunch. It is simply a possibility, a consideration for future study.

A claim that a text t *might* mean such-and-such is simply the statement of an interpretative suggestion, one that admits of many alternative possibilities, and one that remains to be tested by a closer examination of textual evidence. On the other hand, an intepreter might be somewhat more definite about a what a text means. An interpreter may be examining the Book of Daniel. For a variety of reasons, and from a close examination of the text, he may have at least provisionally accepted (1) that the work was initially composed ca. 167-164 B.C., and (2) that its provenance is the resistance movement of the Hasidim. This may suggest to him that at least chapters 1 through 6 of this work *may very well* have an allegorical meaning, one that equates Nebuchadnezzar with Antiochus Epiphanes and which also identifies the incidents or situations in chapters 1 through 6 (allegedly from Nebuchadnezzar's time) with incidents or situations in the time of Antiochus Epiphanes. The work *may very well* present an analysis, in code or allegorical form, of the predicament with which the Hasidim were faced.

The work *may very well* mean this--at least some evidence suggests that it is a fruitful avenue to explore. It all depends on whether or not the proposed equations hold up, how one relates chapters 1 through 6 with the remaining chapters of the work (a problem of unity), and so forth. It, of course, *may very well* not mean this at all. Only a *fuller* exploration of the text will tell. As it stands, it is an interpretation taking shape: textual matters are being explored and an interpretative argument is in the making.

A claim that a text *t may very well* mean such-and-such is one that indicates that an interpretative position has some evidence to support it and that further evidence could or is being gathered to develop it fully. It is not yet a full-blown interpretative argument. It has promise (promise because of evidence, it should be noted).

An interpretative argument is offered, however, when things have gelled--when puzzles in the text, when problems and difficulties in other interpretations of the text, when niggles in one's own understanding of the text have been ironed out. It is an account that emerges when everything "fits," when the pieces come together in a cohesive fashion. An interpretative argument therefore takes shape when the interpreter has "settled" on an interpretation of the text. It represents what the interpreter contends the text *must* mean--*must* mean, that is, according to the evidence taken into account. Interpretative arguments in positions A, B, C, and D are of this nature. They represent "settled" views of what the text *must* mean. Each is offered as an expression of what the text has to mean, given the textual evidence consulted, and each is ready to do battle and match wits with other interpretative positions.

A claim that a text *t must* mean such-and-such is one that indicates that an interpretative argument has been formulated and that an interpretation of the text has been settled upon. The interpretation is, of course, open to revision--revision, that is, in accordance with new evidence or reassessment of old evidence. Such an interpretation is not offered as one of many: it is offered as the text's interpretation.

Question (I), then, should be understood in at least three different senses, depending on how "means" is qualified. So regarded, question (I) may be asking any of the following questions:

(a) what might text *t* mean?
(b) what may text *t* very well mean?
(c) what must text *t* mean?

These are quite different questions, and they call for quite different answers. The answer to question (I) in terms of what a text might mean will be very different from an answer either in terms of what it may very well mean or what it must mean. For one thing, the amount of evidential support one would expect the answer to provide would vary in each instance.

An answer of the form, text t means i_x because ... (where a variety of reasons are cited) is an answer that provides an interpretative argument, one that thereby indicates a settled interpretation of the text. It is an answer, therefore, to question (I) construed as asking, what must text t mean? It is not presented as one in a series of possible meanings not yet fully thought out.

It is for this reason that we can now go back to an answer of form (i) to question (I), a form that posed many interpretative difficulties of its own. I indicated some time ago that some would argue that such an answer is unresponsive. This contention is well founded, for a reason that is now apparent. For to ask question (I) and to receive in reply one or more interpretative arguments is to be confronted with the question in its must-mean sense. To a question that asks, what must text t mean? it would be unresponsive to answer, it means i_1, i_2,...,i_n, for the answer is cast in might-mean or may-very-well-mean terms, senses of "means" that admit of alternative interpretative possibilities.

Incompatible Interpretations

If we understand question (I) as asking what must text t mean? and if we understand interpretative arguments as serious attempts to provide an answer to that question, then certain important consequences follow. For one thing, we would not say that an answer of form (i) to question (I) is all we can expect, for that is precisely the sort of answer we would not expect to the question as so understood. Such an answer would not only not be informative; it would also not be an answer to that question. Secondly, one would therefore not construe the commas in an answer of form (i) as "and" but rather as exclusive "or." One could not remain content with a simple listing of possible meanings. Some selection is indicated. Thirdly, an answer of form (ii) would seem to be more in keeping with question (I) as so understood, although the route to that answer is now seen to be complicated. Selection among rival interpretations would involve the judging of the range of interpretative arguments offered of the text in question, in keeping with the ways in which arguments generally are assessed and in keeping also with any peculiarities concerning interpretative evidence that a detailed study of interpretative arguments may unearth.

This is clearly the case for incompatible interpretations. Where two interpretations of one and the same text are incompatible, say i_x and i_y, there are three possible answers:

(1) neither i_x nor i_y is correct (but another one, namely i_j, is).
(2) one of i_x and i_y is correct, namely....
(3) no interpretation is correct because the text is such that it lacks any one clear meaning.

but not

(4) both i_x and i_y are correct.

(4) is ruled out in the case of incompatibility, for by definition, it cannot be the case that both can be true. We cannot, in this case, appeal either to the richness of the text or to the fecundity of the interpreter's wit and imagination to license interpretative diversity.

Moreover, in the situation of Sophocles' *Oedipus Tyrannus* where two incompatible interpretations are available (namely, the conclusions of arguments A and B), (3) cannot be the case. Options (1) and (2) are the only ones open. In either instance, however, the matter involves settling upon the interpretation of the text, selecting one over others.   The method of that selection has already been indicated.

The situation is the same for all rival interpretations of the same text, all interpretations, that is, that present interpretative arguments in response to question (I) understood as asking what text *t* must mean. The task of interpretative selection cannot be avoided in this instance.

VI

Three things have been done in this paper. We have surveyed several different interpretations of Sophocles' *Oedipus Tyrannus* (including one new one) as an example of an interpretative controversy; we have scouted out a meta-interpretative direction, one that acknowledges the disputative character of textual interpretation; and we have scrutinized several significant ramifications of this, noting, in particular, a pentadic model of interpretation and the central role of interpretative arguments in the study of meta-interpretation. We used interpretations of Sophocles' *Oedipus Tyrannus* to open up a different meta-interpretative direction.

The paper began with a quotation from Jocasta who accuses two arguers--Oedipus and Creon--with having raised a foolish war of words. Interpretation is a war of words (although no foolish one) and it is this aspect on which we have focussed. We have, for the most part, been writing about writing about texts. We never did answer our initial question, what does Sophocles' *Oedipus Tyrannus* mean? But perhaps now we have a sense of what that question means, what some of its complexities involve, and a notion of a direction in which an answer may be found.

Response by Bryant Keeling, Professor of Philosophy
Western Illinois University, Macomb, Illinois

Let me begin by expressing my appreciation to Professor Wilson for one of
the clearest scholarly papers I have ever read. I found his interpretative work
on *Oedipus Tyrannus* very enlightening and his approach to meta-interpretation
provocative. He confronts us with a vast array of hermeneutical questions. He
provides an account of how these questions may arise and why they are important.
Many of the questions he raises are left unanswered. Professor Wilson has chosen
to concentrate on answering a very few questions which are quite basic to hermeneutics. In responding to his paper I shall briefly state what I take to be two
of his main points about meta-interpretation and then I shall indicate why, as an
outsider to the field of hermeneutics, I do not find his arguments for these points
fully convincing.

The two points I wish to discuss here are in fact closely interrelated.
First, Professor Wilson wishes to claim that the interpretation of a text essentially involves argument. An interpretation is always given in a context in which
there is dispute about the meaning of a text (pp. 17-18). Giving one interpretation
of a text involves rejecting other interpretations (p. 18). Therefore, an interpretation stands in need of support by argument (p. 22). Second, Professor Wilson
wishes to claim that unless a text is unclear, there is one and only one correct
interpretation of that text (p. 27). The interpreter is supposed to try to state
what the text *must* mean, not just what it may very well mean (p. 26). These two
claims may initially seem to be fairly modest. I do not know what treatment they
have been given in the recent literature on hermeneutics but I nevertheless find
them somewhat problematic.

Consider Professor Wilson's claim that an interpretation of a text always
stands in need of justification by argument. As Professor Wilson himself tells
us, this immediately raises many questions about the nature of interpretative
argument (p. 24). A fuller consideration of these questions is deferred to a
later paper. Unfortunately, in the absence of clarification of these issues it
is difficult to decide whether or not to agree with the claim Professor Wilson
makes here. I would not be prepared to agree that interpretation essentially
involves argument until I know how narrowly the term "argument" is to be used.
Many different sorts of things are called arguments. Some interpretations of
texts, for example, seem to be descriptions in different words of what they take
the text to be describing. They emphasize some features of the text and deem-
phasize others. Perhaps they suggest ways that certain events described in the
text might have happened or be understood to have happened. They seem to be
appealing to the reader to "see" that this is what the text is saying. Are we
to call this argument? Sometimes such procedures *are* called arguments. If the
term "argument" is to be used broadly enough to include procedures like the one I
have just described, then Professor Wilson's claim seems to be true but relatively
uninteresting.

I am inclined to think, however, that Professor Wilson has a rather narrower use of the term "argument" in mind. While he never tells us that procedures
of the sort I have described above are not to be called arguments, he does concentrate his attentions on interpretations that involve arguments in a narrower
sense. Note the way he lays out the interpretations of *Oedipus Tyrannus* in the
first half of his paper. Here we are given something like traditional arguments
with premises and conclusions. Let us assume for the moment that he wishes to

make the rather more interesting claim that a given interpretation of a text stands in need of support by argument in some restricted sense of the term "argument" (to be specified at a later time). We cannot fully evaluate the claim until we know what this restricted sense is, but we can at least ask whether the claim is intended to be descriptive or normative. If the claim is meant to be descriptive, the interpretative procedure which I described above would seem to constitute a counter-example which would show the claim to be false. If, on the other hand, the claim is meant to be normative, Professor Wilson must explain why interpreters should make use of arguments in his sense of the term. He cannot, I think, defend this claim by saying that only by the use of this kind of argument will disputes about interpretations finally be resolved. In fact such disputes are sometimes settled without such arguments and often remain unsettled even when such arguments are used profusely. Perhaps there is some other way to proceed here. We must have further explanation by Professor Wilson before we can make a judgment. Nevertheless, I am inclined to be skeptical at this point that a case can be made that interpretation *should* use argument (in some narrow sense of argument) rather than relying on, for example, rich description and an appeal to the reader to "see" that this is what the text means.

Now let us consider Professor Wilson's claim that unless a text is unclear, there is one and only one correct interpretation of that text. Perhaps I have not grasped the point he is trying to make here but this claim seems to me to be true but relatively inconsequential. He explicitly says that he is considering the case where we have *incompatible* claims and, as he points out, by definition two incompatible claims cannot both be correct. If we admit that two interpretations are incompatible, then we cannot say they are both correct. If we say that two interpretations are both correct, then we cannot say that they are incompatible. Professor Wilson also says that there may be texts which lack any one clear meaning and therefore have no "correct" interpretation (p. 60). What are we to make of this? Apart from *establishing* a correct interpretation (and what does "correct" mean here?) is there any way to tell whether a text has one clear meaning? If not, then the existence of multiple incompatible interpretations can always be cited as a reason for saying that the text has no one clear meaning. In this case perhaps some literary critics would want to say that *all* important texts are such that they lack one clear meaning. Maybe this rich diversity of interpretation could even be used as a criterion for the importance of a text. What, for example, should we say about *Oedipus Tyrannus*? If we admit that interpretations A and B are incompatible, then we certainly shouldn't say that they are both correct. But should we say, perhaps, that since various plausible interpretations of *Oedipus Tyrannus* have been offered and there is no consensus as to which one is correct, *Oedipus Tyrannus* has no one clear meaning? In this case couldn't the question, "What does *Oedipus Tyrannus* mean?" be answered, "*Oedipus Tyrannus* means interpretation A. interpretation B, interpretation C, etc."? I do not see how Professor Wilson's second claim can be used to move meta-interpretation beyond the pluralism he seems to deplore. I do not know whether there are major figures in the fields of hermeneutics who espouse the form of pluralism of interpretations which he rejects, but if there are, I believe he will have to state and defend a stronger claim than he does to drive their position from the field. They need only to refrain from using the word "correct" to describe the interpretations of a text and the expression "has one clear meaning" to describe the text and they can continue as before. It is not clear to me that from their perspective they would necessarily be giving up anything of importance.

At this point I cannot resist the temptation to indicate my suspicion (and it is no more than that) that Professor Wilson's paper grows out of a desire on his part to assimilate textual interpretations to scientific explanation of natural phenomena. No doubt he would recognize that there are many differences between the two, but in both cases there is an objective reality to be understood, there are various understandings which have been advanced, and there is need for a way of deciding among these understandings. In the case of scientific explanation of natural phenomena some would say: (1) such explanations always stand in need of support by argument, and (2) there is one and only one correct explanation of the phenomena being explained. Now consider Professor Wilson's statement that his view ". . . places hermeneutics directly in the same sort of square of controversy in which other kinds of disputes--e.g., legal, academic, scientific, moral, governmental, etc.--find expression, challenge, and perhaps eventual resolution" (p. 23). Initially I found this passage quite puzzling. If, as I am inclined to think, the disputes involved in all of the areas he mentions have little more in common than that they are all called "disputes," then it is not very enlightening to place hermeneutical disputes among them. What dispute doesn't belong among them? My guess is that Professor Wilson takes disputes about scientific explanation (or something rather like them) as paradigmatic and thinks that it is already clear that the other kinds of disputes mentioned (legal, academic, moral, etc.) already fit this model.

If something like this is the case, then, of course, a host of new problems arise. There is, as far as I can see, no consensus among philosophers of science about how scientific disputes are to be resolved or even about whether all scientific disputes are of a single type. Nor is it clear that all would agree that there is one and only one correct scientific explanation of a given phenomenon. In addition, it is hard to see how someone could argue that this paradigm (or one like it) *should* be applied in the area of textual interpretation (even if the paradigm could be established). Some might wish to maintain, for example, that textual interpretation is itself more like art than like science.

Response by Hans Ulrich Gumbrecht, Professor of Romance Literature
University of the Ruhr, Bochum, West Germany; and Visiting Professor of French,
University of California, Berkeley

I wonder whether Barrie Wilson's essay on "meta-interpretation" (and more particularly his "pentadic model") is to be understood as a theory concerning *any form of text-guided sense-making* (i.e., interpretation), or as a model of a very special type of it, the "scholarly" interpretation (cf. pp. 22 & 21).

(I) If the first assumption is true, I would object that the situation of (interpretative) *conflict* and the textual form it brings about ("*argument*") are not characteristic for most of the acts we call "interpretation."

(II) If the pentadic model refers only to the scholarly interpretation, I would admit that it gives an adequate description of most of what we call "criticism" within the realm of the Humanities; but I would also ask *if the Humanities can afford* to proceed in the way Wilson's theory gives an image of.

I

It is not the existence of alternative interpretations which makes scholarly interpretation use the textual form of "argument"; the very first scholarly interpretations of any text will try as hard to be convincing (and what we call "argumentation" is all the devices related to this intention) as the series of the following interpretations. The intention to convince is always due to a type of communicative situation the central feature of which is lack of evidence, and argumentation is a means of reducing this lack of evidence to certainty. Now the reason for the lack of evidence in the situation of scholarly interpretation is the knowledge (or the worrying) of scholars about the fact that different meanings can be conveyed from any text. This knowledge (or this fear) is part of our specific professional competence.

As part of a specific competence we cannot assume their belonging to that part of everyday-knowledge (in Husserl's and Alfred Schuetz' sense) which guides interpretative acts (not only of texts) in our everyday-life. In fact: unless opposition rises, texts appear ambiguous, or everyday-competence is insufficient, the meaning one believes to be "in" the text is found with the same certainty as, for example, colors are attributed to those phenomena which become objects of our perception. There is no general lack of evidence in the situation of everyday-interpretation because there are always questions and attitudes (*Fragestellungen und Einstellungen*) under which we read or hear the texts, and with which they fit.

This fact seems to be obvious for anybody--except for scholars who have a strange and stubborn tendency of projecting their own professional style of reception into the historical situations of communication they are dealing with. Scholarly "histories of the reception" of (mostly) literary texts furnish abundant examples. Reading them one becomes familiar with the impression that readers or audiences of the past were in a continuous competition with each previous reception-group, seeking with sophisticated arguments those meanings the texts contained as answers to their very special questions, or trying, within a process of historical accumulation, to reveal their entire "semantical treasures." I don't think, however, that what can be considered historically particular features of understanding the Bible in the twelfth century or of enjoying Shakespeare's dramas in the nineteenth century was conditioned to any important extent by preceding interpretations. Horizons of expectation or dispositions of reception by non-scholarly audiences and readers depend much less on alternative ways of understanding than on stocks of everyday experience (which historiography can present us as historically specific but) which readers of the past would have taken as, let us say, "generally human."

Wilson's essay offers no evidence to the issue of whether he shares the (above mentioned) scholarly attitude of holding the scholarly type of interpretation to be "generally human," or whether he wants the pentadic model to be exclusively related to the business of professional critics. If it is meant to be a model in the second (restricted) sense, then he should inform his readers about such an intended meaning; a restriction of its field of application would by no means reduce the relevance of his theory, but it would show which use we can make of it.

II

It may be a very typically German expectation which was guiding my reading of Wilson's essay. I refer to the expectation that a philosophical contribution to the theory of interpretation should (at least) not only be descriptive but also be normative. There are two reasons to say that Wilson's essay is unfortunately only descriptive: (1) because scholarly interpretation unfortunately is mostly just like the pentadic model tells us; and (2) because Wilson unfortunately doesn't give any orientation about how that situation can be changed (or about why he doesn't think that there is any need for changing it).

The pentadic model points out (and the traditional scholarly interpretation believes) that interpretative positions are supported by interpretative reasons which, by their turn, ground in textual evidence (cf. p. 23). Such a procedure presupposes that any text has but one (or, but a limited number of) meaning(s) "by itself" in which such evidence can be found. There should, however, be no dispute about the experience that "texts by themselves" become only meaningful when related to the social knowledge (the communicative competence) of those who use them as means of interaction, and that any texts can be related to many different such competences. Wolfgang Iser's model of "the act of reading" shows in detail how "sense" or "meaning" is the outcome of the dialectic relation between text and knowledge. It is the (author's or the) reader's knowledge which attributes to each of the words which a text contains one of the meanings they can stand for (a fact which is the theoretical condition of what in Germany is called "Begriffsgeschichte"), which chooses one of the often multiple possibilities of combining its sentences (or chapters), which provides the background which the text needs to become an "answer" or a "question" or whatever speech act. What has been said is true for any text, and it should even become more obvious for readers of those texts to which different societies and different ages gave different meanings.

The interesting issue is in the question why scholars have such a clear tendency to deny this trivial fact, why they present their interpretations indeed as statements about "what the text must mean," and not of "what the text must mean

in relation to a specific knowledge/competence." I find three possible answers:
(a) Scholars are, unbelievable as it sounds, naive enough--but who, among scholars,
would really believe that? (b) Scholars have good reasons (related to profession
and status) to dismiss the fact of any text's polysemantic character--although no
particular scholar can be blamed for doing so, because this dismissing has become
an obligatory part of his professional socialization. (c) Scholars do know that
texts adopt meanings only in relation to knowledge/competence, but they also know
that they all share an identical knowledge/competence, which makes unnecessary
keeping it in mind--a hypothesis too ideal to be true. As I have no ambition of
entering in a kind of psycho-criticism of criticism, I won't argue about the rela-
tive probability of these three explanations; but I will try to show why scholarly
interpretation cannot afford reproducing this very special attitude toward its
own achievements.

Only by keeping in mind the changing stocks of knowledge/competence which
are (as much as the text itself) a requirement for meaning can we approach the
crucial issue of who might be the potential addressees of our interpretations.
This question is by no means a particular problem of (German) Protestant theology,
as Wilson seems to presuppose. On the contrary: if Bultmann's contribution to
the hermeneutic tradition became a model for other disciplines within the Humanities, this happened because he underlined the fact that the polysemantic character of texts did not necessarily lead to arbitrariness in interpretation, but
had to be taken as a stimulus for thinking about its functions, its aims, i.e.,
about its addressees. This is the level where I would locate "argumentation"
within the complex act of scholarly interpretation; its frame of reference is,
instead of textual evidence, that part of philosophy which we call "ethics."
Returning for a moment to the formula with which Wilson describes the scholars'
attitude to scholarly interpretation, we can now again say that proposals for
meaning can be forwarded as statements about "what the text *must* mean"; "must,"
however, no longer refers to a pretended logical relation between text and meaning,
but to the responsibility which any non-private interpretation implies.

What makes the situation of (e.g.) literary criticism different from the
communicative frames of theology is the fact that its direct addressees are
more frequently to be found among fellow-critics or neighbor-disciplines instead
of non-professional readers. But even if its "application" is less immediate, it
has to be taken into consideration. If an interpretation of Shakespeare's theater
in relation to its contemporary audience is meant to be a contribution to social
history, then we have--simply and pathetically--to ask what research in social
history is for. There are, of course, no metahistorical norms for the normative
orientation ("application") of interpretation; the obligatory argumentation about
this issue never comes to an end.

So my final question is, whether forgetting about the polysemantic character of texts as part of scholarly interpretation is not a price for which we get
rid of this very obligation, and, whether we can really afford this bargain.

Response by Marvin Brown, Lecturer in Religion and Society
Graduate Theological Union, Berkeley

I agree with Professor Wilson's emphasis upon the argumentative character of textual interpretation, and in my response, I would like to examine the relationship between argumentation and the interpretive situation.

Professor Wilson proposes that the interpretive situation be understood as involving five elements (p. 21) with its argumentative component residing in the relationship between the interpreter and other interpreters of the same text, or between my interpretation and other interpretations of the same text. This location of the basis for argument seems unduly restrictive. Even though one may interpret a text with other interpretations in mind, such as Knox's or Vellacott's in the case of *Oedipus Tyrannus*, one's appeal, more than likely, will be to a larger community who will judge, in the course of time, which interpretation is more convincing. In other words, interpreters address not only other interpreters of the same text, but also, to use Josiah Royce's phrase, a "community of interpretation." Instead of limiting the addresses to any particular group, it seems more helpful to say that interpreters of texts have "implied audiences" much as texts have "implied audiences," and that the particular "audience" of any interpretation can be discovered through the kinds of arguments that one uses to gain assent to the interpretation. From this view, "implied audience" and "argument" are bound very closely together.

As Aristotle has said, we argue about things that are debatable. We also argue about things upon which we have disagreements and agreements. The disagreements give us reason to argue. The agreements provide the basis for arguing. A community of interpretation exists because of the shared agreements and perspectives that provide the common ground for the give and take of argumentation. Every interpreter construes a community of interpretation or "audience," sometimes naively and sometimes thoughtfully. In either case, the "community" provides essential materials for the construction of arguments.

In many instances of interpretation we find that the interpreter has a multitude of different possible "audiences." For example, in the interpretation of the law, the judge may address other legal interpreters, or the litigants, or the general public. Which one he takes as primary will affect his "reading" of the text and the reasons he gives for his judgment. Pincoffs' analysis of these different audiences led him to the following observation:

> Retributionists tend to speak as if the judge had
> only the audience of litigants; utilitarians as if
> he spoke to the general audience alone; traditional-
> ists as if the judge's obligation to his judicial
> ancestors were the sole obligation which binds him.[1]

Pincoffs' observation leads one to question any simple notion of "fidelity to the text." In the case of interpreting the law, should one be faithful to the text?

---

[1]Edmond Pincoffs, "The Audiences of the Judge," *Logique et Analyse* (Mar-Juin 1961) 343.

to other interpretations? to the litigants? or to the general public? This does become rather complex. For example, I suppose that Barth's biblical interpretations show a stronger fidelity to the text and Bultmann's show a stronger fidelity to "modern" persons, or perhaps the differences in their interpretations show that they had different audiences "in mind." In any case, the selection of audiences and the placement of fidelity will determine the perception of "evidence" for developing an interpretation. In fact, the discernment of different audiences and fidelities might explain some of the apparent conflicts in interpretations.

From this perspective of "audiences" and "fidelities" we can now look at the question of "interpretative arguments." Professor Wilson proposes that the central locus for examining the strength of such arguments is in the relationship between the interpretation and the text (p. 23). I think this tends to de-contextualize the actual process of interpretation. Let us return to legal hermeneutics where "evidence" plays an essential role. In a typical case, various kinds of evidence from the situation are presented and then in "conversation" with the evidence of the text, one interprets the law. "What the text means" in this situation will depend upon the selection and organizing of evidence, and if a "new" meaning is discovered, it will emerge from a new crystallization of situational and textual evidence. Furthermore, when the judge defends his interpretation, he may well use the evidence presented in the case as support for his understanding of "what the text means" in this situation. I think this "conversation" between text and situation applies to other regional hermeneutics as well, even though other interpreters do not have the giving of testimony in the same manner. In other words, interpretative arguments belong to interpretive situations, and their strength will depend upon their selection and organizing of the available "means of persuasion" in a particular situation. The text itself is certainly one of these means, but not the only one.

Response by Joseph Fontenrose, Professor of Classics, Emeritus
University of California, Berkeley

Professor Wilson's paper raises important hermeneutic questions about the interpretation of any text and illustrates them mainly by consideration of *Oedipus Tyrannus*. My interest is chiefly in the interpretation of this play.

Wilson offers interpretations A (Bernard Knox), B (his own), C ("somewhat facetious"), D (Vellacott). All of these are wrong, I would say. B is faulty in particulars, e.g., the estimation of the chorus's role as merely passive and uncomprehending. It does not attribute the plague to Ares' activity. In verse 190 *Ares* is simply metaphorical, used by metonymy for the plague. The chorus represents the citizens of Thebes, who, like any Greek citizen-body, pray for divine assistance in a time of disaster; they are not rejecting inquiry in favor of divine assistance (p. 9). And B's basic interpretation is at best dubious, that the play is concerned with the difference between appearance and reality. Of course, Oedipus finds out that things are not what they at first seem, or rather, that the truth is not what he supposed it to be. But this is incidental to the plot, and Sophocles is surely not illustrating Parmenides.

There are other interpretations of *OT* too--E, F, G, H, and on to Z. There is the traditional view that it is a tragedy of fate (e.g., Mandel). To this we can make the Aristotelian objection that the tragic *peripateia* cannot be that of a good man reduced from good fortune to bad; that is merely shocking. We have tragedy only when a man of high position, not eminently virtuous (but by no means wicked), more good than bad, falls from his high position through a flaw of character, *hamartia*. And in this very sentence Aristotle names Oedipus as an example.

But though one can certainly find faults in Oedipus' character, it is difficult to find a fault that caused his downfall. There are the oracles that predicted what he would do, and that is what he did. Yet we not only consider *OT* a tragedy, but we also commonly consider it the very model of a tragedy. As Freud has said, the characterization of *OT* as a tragedy of fate does not explain why it has moved ancient and modern audiences alike.

Critics have pointed out Oedipus' faults (Whitman, Kitto) like irascibility, ill-considered action, overconfidence, pride, conceit, blindness of soul. But these do not seem to have led directly to his doom, unless one says that his persistent search for the murderer of Laios was a mistake, as does Dorothea Krook. For her, "Oedipus' passionate search for the truth about himself...is a search for self-knowledge. When it is as relentless and uncompromising as Oedipus', when it will stop at nothing to get at the truth, it is a form of the quest for the forbidden Faustian kind of knowledge." As everyone knows, we should not emulate Faust. But would it be better that Oedipus refuse to look for the murderer of Laios, which led to his inquiry into his origins, when according to Apollo's oracle only finding the murderer and punishing him would end the plague that gripped the city?

There are those who read the issue as order against disorder. Oedipus' patricide and incest have violated the cosmic order, which must be set right (Kitto, Bowra). For Bowra the gods have selected Oedipus from before his birth as an example to teach mankind a salutary lesson, and they teach the lesson through Oedipus' own gifts. The humbling of Oedipus teaches men that they cannot trust in their happiness or knowledge; the gods can end it in a moment. That is, the gods have Oedipus kill his father and marry his mother in order to ruin him eventually and teach mankind a lesson. This seems to put the gods in a bad light. As Waldock says, if this is what Sophocles intended, he "has been wasting our time." Bowra's interpretation has some similarities to Knox's (Wilson's A).

Others (Waldock, Vaughan) reject any attempt to find meaning in *OT*. Waldock says that it is a well-constructed drama; that is all. Vaughan lauds Sophocles as a consummate master of plot.

For me, the question of how to interpret *OT* is inseparable from the question of what constitutes the tragedy of Oedipus. I shall venture (as briefly as possible) upon an Aristotelian interpretation of *OT*, attempting to show exactly what is Oedipus' *hamartia* and to show exactly what is the play's tragic effect on us. What is the essence of the tragedy of Oedipus the King?

At the outset we see Oedipus supremely confident in his position and power. When he hears the oracle that the slayer of Laios is in Thebes and must be banished or killed he doesn't imagine that he himself can be the killer. He sets out to find the culprit and after much harrowing inquiry finds that it is himself, and not only that he killed Laios, but that Laios was also his father, and that in marrying Laios' widow he married his own mother. Thus the prophecy that he received at Delphi years before is proved true, and the curse that he put upon the murderer's head has come down on his own.

This fall from confident power to ruin through self-discovery moves us certainly, and we can see that Oedipus is initially overconfident, proud, self-engrossed. And you may well agree that his is moving, but still question whether it is enough in itself to be the whole tragic effect. And it is not all: to Oedipus' initial confidence we must add his culpability in feeling it. Oedipus was not justified in feeling so much confidence, especially after he had heard Teiresias speak.

At 715-716 Jocasta tells Oedipus that bandits killed Laios at *triplai hamaxitai*. This at once strikes Oedipus; it recalls an event that occurred before he came to Thebes: he had killed a man at that very place. This really begins the inquiry that leads to self-discovery. In the following lines and in 103-131 it is evident that Oedipus knew nothing about Laios or what had happened to him, although he had come to Thebes just after Laios' death, which he had caused. It is no good to say that the surviving servant told the Thebans that robbers had killed Laios, and that the plural put Oedipus off, although he had killed a man at the very place just before. The plural does not put him off years later, and apparently he has now for the first time heard of the crossroads as the murder scene.

The oracles spoken to Laios and Oedipus, the patricide, and the incest are events precedent to the drama. Yet obviously they are factors that affect it. We must look at the oracle spoken to Oedipus. He had been taunted by a drinking companion, who said that Oedipus was not really the son of Polybos and Merope. The taunt bothered Oedipus, and he went to his putative parents, who reassured him that he was really their son. But he was still not satisfied; the doubt preyed upon him, and so he went to Delphi to ask who his parents were. The god replied that he was destined to kill his father and marry his mother--the later verse form adds that he should not return to his native land. At this point Oedipus immediately forgot the question that had been bothering him so much, the very question that he had just put to the Pythia, and immediately assumed that Polybos and Merope were his real parents (and that Corinth was his native land). He decided not to return to Corinth and went off in a different direction. At the three-way crossroads that same day he had an altercation with a man old enough to be his father--moreover who resembled himself--and in ungovernable wrath killed him and three of his attendants. He seems to have thought nothing of this, but to have gone on his way rejoicing, and so came to Thebes, answered the riddle of the Sphinx, took the throne, and married the dead king's widow, old enough to be his mother. Thus he returned to his native land, having killed his father, and there married his mother.

Then, it appears, he was wholly incurious about his predecessor. He learned nothing about him until this day, many years later. Teiresias reveals the whole truth to him in terms (366-367) that should have recalled Apollo's oracle spoken to him. But Oedipus is too angry to listen. Teiresias, he should know, is an infallible seer, but he can only accuse him of conspiracy. Then when Jocasta tells him the oracle that Laios had received before his birth, he fails to perceive that it is strikingly similar to that which he received and which he mentions fewer than eighty lines later; it merely lacks the incest prophecy. In the whole inquiry from that point on he is painfully slow at putting the pieces together. Jocasta realizes the truth long before he does, and so does the audience (even if it has no previous knowledge of the story).

So the tragedy of Oedipus lies not only in his fall from power and in the complete dissipation of his initial confidence in his position and innocence, but also in the irrationality and indefensibility of his confidence; for the knowledge was available to him from the outset. In a sense, Vellacott is right: Oedipus knew all the time. Here is Oedipus' *hamartia*, his hybris: he was hasty, incurious, incautious, arrogant, stubborn, unreflective, blind of soul. But can we say that this *hamartia* led to his downfall? He had already committed patricide and incest. These deeds and the oracles belong to the myth that Sophocles dramatized.

Still, we may take Knox's suggestion and imagine the play without the oracles. Suppose--no oracle having been spoken to anyone--that Oedipus, having to find the murderer of Laios, finds that he himself is the culprit, and also that Laios was his father, and that he had married his mother. We would say, I am sure, that Oedipus had acted rashly and wrongly in his encounter with the old man at the crossroads, that his subsequent unconcern and amnesia were reprehensible (he had just killed a man, in fact four men), and that his confidence in his power and in his innocence was unjustified. The same flaw of character that led him to kill Laios and to marry his mother before the play begins is reenacted in the inquiry that leads to his discovery of what he had done. So without the oracles and without the gods his flaw(s) and his guilt would be evident. But we have the oracles. Notice, however, that they are primarily warnings to Laios and Oedipus: if the warnings are not heeded, then the consequences will be as predicted. Oedipus could have avoided his fate.

So I take the interpretative position that Wilson labels (ii), that t means i_x, this being the interpretation made above. I will qualify this by saying that any compatible interpretation can be joined to it. It differs from compatible interpretations in emphasis; each, we may say, is a valid interpretation.

Now how do I arrive at this interpretation? From close study of the text, of every word and sentence spoken, getting at the intention of every speech, and relating one speech to another, one dialogue to another, and each episode to every other (and this demands a good understanding of Sophocles' Greek). That is, it adheres strictly *to the evidence*. This is what Wilson's meta-interpretative inquiry boils down to-- "It puts the onus on the interpreters to defend their interpretative reasons and to challenge the differing interpretative reasons of others--*by the evidence*" (p. 23).

The meaning we must find is Sophocles' meaning, unless we are going to say that the text has meanings which Sophocles did not intend. And in finding his meaning we must not go *ektos tou logou*; we must strictly avoid what Waldock has called the documentary fallacy, which is to treat a literary composition as though it were an historical document and to take unmentioned events and factors into account. This does not rule out all extra-textual considerations (p. 24); e.g., the meaning of a word, phrase, or sentence may be clarified from information about the author and his times--we do have to know all that the author intends.

For the rest I have a few random comments to make.

How does the pentadic "model" of interpretation suit the situation of the first interpreter? He is not interpreting in a "context of other interpreters who have provided their interpretations of the same text."

Oedipus' accusation of Kreon shows anything but "the alacrity and astuteness of Oedipus' logical mind" (p. 10). It rather reveals faults of Oedipus' character, irascibility and hasty judgment. Logical is one thing that Oedipus' mind is not. And is it true that the alternative to supposing Kreon at fault is his own guilt? Kreon could be honest even if Teiresias' statement is false.

Wilson takes poetic language too literally when, as evidence of the chorus' obtuseness, he points to *OT* 1213,

$$\text{ἐφηῦρέ σ᾽ ἄκονθ᾽ ὁ πάνθ᾽ ὁρῶν χρόνος}$$

saying that the chorus is off-target (p. 11): time didn't find Oedipus out, but Oedipus himself. All the chorus means is that after a long time Oedipus and everyone else has learned the truth about him.

Can we say that Teiresias' perception of the truth is only true opinion, not knowledge? In *OT* Teiresias speaks for the gods; and who would have knowledge, if not the gods?

Response by Mark Griffith, Associate Professor of Classics
University of California, Berkeley

Interpretation involves explaining, revealing, or transmitting meaning that is
otherwise concealed or obscure. The nature and manner of this interpretation may be
of many kinds, according to the kind of meaning that we are looking for.[1] Critics are
notoriously disinclined to agree what constitutes "the meaning" of, e.g., a painting
or a symphony, and even in the case of literature, where the words might be expected
to signify something quite specific and paraphrasable, it appears that "few contemporary aestheticians argue that it is in principle possible to discover 'the correct interpretation' of a text."[2] This must be because they do not believe that there *is* a
single meaning to be explained; I think that this disbelief is correct.

Literary fiction occupies a place somewhere between representational painting
or sculpture on the one hand, and philosophical argument or ordinary discourse on the
other. Literary critics fall broadly into two classes. Some concentrate on the form
of a text, and interpret (i.e., reveal and explain) its nature and function in terms
of the relationship of the parts to each other and to the whole, or in terms of the
effect that this formal arrangement makes on the reader or audience. Others prefer
to concentrate on the things in the real world that are signified by the words of the
text, and to interpret the content, i.e., "what the author is trying to say."[3] It is
obvious that the meaning of Sophocles' *OT* will be different for each of these groups
of critics.

Professor Wilson (henceforth W.) clearly belongs to the second group. The meaning that he seeks in his interesting paper is essentially its message, i.e., its content as separable from its form.[4] Thus the four interpretations of *OT* which he advances
(two serious, two more or less frivolous) are in the form of propositions about the nature of human existence:

A (W. p. 18 = Knox pp. 42-3) "The play *is a* terrifying *affirmation* of the
truth of prophecy...", or, more expansively, "The play *is a reassertion* of the religious view of a divinely ordered universe...."

B (W. p. 13 = Wilson himself) *OT is a story about* the dreadful agony of human
inquiry...."

_____

[1]My definition of "interpretation" is based on the *OED*. On the problem of what
interpretation can or should mean, and what "meaning" means, I have been helped most
by the following: Wallace Martin *art*. "Interpretation, modern", in *Princeton Encyclo-
pedia of Poetry and Poetics*, ed. A. Preminger (enlarged ed. 1974) 943-947; M. C. Beardsley *art*. "Metacriticism," *ibid*. 951-5; M. Krieger *art*. "Meaning, problem of", *ibid*.
475-9; M. C. Beardsley, "The limits of critical interpretation", in Sidney Hook, ed.,
Art and philosophy (New York 1966); S. Hampshire, "Types of interpretation", *ibid*;
I. A. Richards, *Principles of literary criticism* (1924, New York 1959); R. S. Crane,
The language of criticism and the structure of poetry (Toronto 1953).

[2]Martin (see n. 1), p. 946.

[3]See the articles of, e.g., Beardsley and Hofstadter in Hook (ed.), above n. 1.

[4]This is termed by him "exegesis   p. 1, fairly enough, I think.

C (W. p. 13 = Wilson$_2$, tongue-in-cheek) "The play *shows the superiority* of intuitive reasoning over methodical deduction...."

D (W. p. 14, based on Vellacott p. 104) "The play *becomes...a study* of the terror of admitting to oneself and to others the truth about oneself...."

(In each case I have added the emphasis, to bring out the redefinition of *OT* as an affirmation, a story, a demonstration, or a study, rather than as a poem or drama.)

A, B, C, and D are examples of the kinds of answers that W. expects to his "naive" question (p. 4), "What is the meaning of *OT*?" The underlying assumption is, that we should be able to make a single statement summing up the main philosophical conclusions or implications contained in the text. W.'s inquiry in Parts IV and V of his paper is then intended to discover whether more than one such statement can be wholly true and adequate for the same text; in particular, whether it is possible for two conflicting statements of this kind both to be true; and if they cannot, how we are to distinguish true, or truer, statements from less true.

Before I go on to discuss W.'s treatment of this problem, and of *OT* itself, I should express some of my reservations about the validity of the simple question, "What is the meaning of *OT*?," and of the kinds of propositions that are offered in response. Most tragedies, surely, are not designed by their authors, nor expected by their audiences, *primarily* to convey philosophical, religious, political, etc. opinions or propositions. They may do more of this than a painting or symphony or game of chess, insofar as they deal more directly with people, actions, and issues resembling the real world: but, like those other works of art, they win our interest, satisfaction, and pleasure in large part from the formal arrangement (plot) and means of expression (poetical language, plus, in some cases, scenery, music, dance, etc.), and not simply from the message that can be extracted from them.

Any account of *OT* which makes no mention of the formal symmetry and neatness of its structure is, I think, deficient, in that it ignores the effect made by this structure. There is significance, not just in *what* happens in *OT*, but in *how* it happens. The discovery of the truth about Oedipus is horrifying, in that it brings him pain, but comforting, in that it satisfies our expectations aroused since early in the play by Sophocles' techniques of foreshadowing and dramatic irony. We might conclude (more or less with Nietzsche) that, whereas the paraphrasable content of *OT* seems to demonstrate the futility of human endeavour and the chaotic and nauseating horror of our existence, the structure and poetry of the play serve simultaneously to reassure us that harmony and order *do* indeed prevail, and that even the sufferings of an Oedipus can be turned into an object of beauty and comfort. Nietzsche and others thus look for aesthetic, rather than moral or religious meaning in a tragedy; or rather, for them aesthetic criteria have acquired a moral value, and human life is valued for art's sake. We need not go so far as this; but we should give due weight to the effect made by the dynamics and structure of a drama, and not limit our assessment of it exclusively to the paraphrasable content. In short, I am suggesting that "exegetical interpretation" of the kind practised by W. is less obviously appropriate to a literary text than to a piece of expository or protreptic discourse; and among literary texts, it is less obviously appropriate to a tragedy than, e.g., to a didactic poem or satire. [5]

---

[5] See especially Crane (n. 1) passim.

It is particularly important to bear in mind that, unlike a philosopher or moralist or politician, a playwright does not speak in his own voice. He is thus under no obligation to present a univocal, or even self-consistent view of the events that he is presenting on stage.[6] Likewise he need not point any moral, or draw conclusions, that can be extracted from the play and given as an adequate summary of the play's message. If we were to ask the naive question, "What was the meaning of the Vietnam War?", we should expect quite different answers from a U. S. politician, a Viet Cong guerilla, and a disabled G.I. veteran. So too, the action of *OT* means something different to Creon, to Teiresias, to the citizens of Thebes, and to Oedipus. None of these characters can be identified with Sophocles himself; and none of them commands our own total identification with them during the play or after it. As we witness and share the experiences of all these characters, we may find several different meanings in the same actions and words, according to our shifting perspective. That is what drama is like; that is how it works.

It should be clear by now that I tend to favor the "tetradic" model of W. (p. 20), which includes reference to the reader/spectator in the process of interpretation. (Indeed, the definition of the word "interpretation" seems to me to require such reference.) But here I am anxious only to insist on two preliminary points, which are not raised by W.: (1) "Exegetical" interpretation of a drama conveys and explains only one aspect of its meaning (just as the exegesis of a painting may explain, e.g., the religious or political significance of its symbols, and may succeed in paraphrasing its content and perhaps in suggesting the intentions of the painter, without taking account of form, color, composition, etc.); (2) The nature of tragedy (as of several other kinds of poetry) is such as to allow multiple meanings within the same text. Paradox, ambiguity, perhaps even self-contradiction, are admissible and effective, whereas they would not be in expository prose or even didactic poetry. There is no reliable way of determining what is the primary meaning of a text which plainly allows for, even aims at, such ambiguity and richness of texture. Likewise, a tragedy may convey or imply several different *kinds* of meaning: there may be a political, a religious, a psychological "message", each quite distinct--or not--from each other. Interpretation will be able to reveal each of these different kinds of meaning; but none will contradict the others, since each interpretation will be an answer to a different question about the play. Sometimes the play itself may make clear where its primary area of concern lies (politics, religion, etc.); more often, in tragedy, it will not, and argument as to the primary or true meaning, out of these several meanings, will be vain.

My assumption, then, is that it *is* true of most literary texts that t means i_1 *and* i_2, etc. (= i_n, W. p. 15), insofar as there are n *kinds* of meaning which may be predicated of it (political, religious, etc.). In such cases, i_1 in no way conflicts with i_2; they are quite compatible, as answers to different questions about the play. I assume too that, in a trivial sense, every reader/spectator finds his own private meaning in every text; and however poorly grounded in the text and solipsistic his view

---

[6] If space permitted, I would here discuss two examples of ambiguous or multi-levelled meanings of other literary works; Hesiod *Works and Days* 202-212, the Fable or Parable of the Hawk and the Nightingale, which seems to contain three messages, one for unenlightened kings, one for enlightened kings, and perhaps one for peasants (and Perses, Hesiod's brother). Only the context of the rest of the poem, and Hesiod's clearly didactic stance, makes clear which meaning he regards as being the truest; and Kafka's Parable towards the end of *The Trial*, which admits of numerous valid, but incompatible, interpretations which are never resolved.

may appear to others, we cannot really deny that this *is* the meaning of the text *to hi*
--though we may hope that he may abondon this meaning in favor of another, if a good
critic interprets the text to him properly (i.e., in better accord with what the text
actually says). With these qualifications made, we still have to face the problem
raised in the body of W.'s paper: What are we to do when faced with contradictory answers to the *same kind* of question about a text? How do we choose one interpretation
over another? Or can we allow both to stand?

The natural response (which it seems to me W. accepts) is that we make up our
minds by using the usual methods of argument and rules of evidence. Thus, in the case
of two rival interpretations of *OT*, we should first examine both to see whether they
are in accord with the text; if they are, we must then see whether they are really, or
only apparently, incompatible with each other. Only if both turn out to be equally
true to the text, and yet incompatible as philosophical propositions, do we have a rea᷾
problem, and we may be compelled to recognize that the text is paradoxical or self-con-
tradictory in respect to this question that we have asked of it. In the case of the
interpretations of *OT* discussed by W., I do not think that we are driven to such a conclusion, as I will try to show.

Interpretations A and B of *OT* (outlined by W. in pp. 4-18) are both intended to
answer the (implied) question, "What do we learn from *OT* about the effectiveness of the
human intellect in providing happiness or in truly understanding the world we live in?"
Answer A (Knox, W. p. 18) asserts that we learn that the human intellect is largely ineffectual and misguided in its efforts to improve human life, in the face of an inscru-
table divine will which reveals itself only through inspired prophecy. Answer B (W. p.
13) asserts that human inquiry *does* provide greater understanding, though at a horrible
price. If we accept that such improved understanding is desirable, then these two answers are incompatible. Certainly the steps in the argument leading to both contain
incompatible propositions (A6 and B3, W. p. 7, p. 12, cf. p. 17). Are they both equall
well supported by the text? I think not. Knox's description of Oedipus' behavior is
quite lopsided; by concentrating on Oedipus' attempts to avoid killing his supposed
father and marrying his supposed mother, and on his natural, almost inescapable, conclusion that certain divine prophecies have turned out false, Knox tries to represent
Oedipus as "like the person...who scoffs at religion, who favors arrogant humanism..."
etc. (Knox p. 42 = A6, W. p. 7). But this involves ignoring Oedipus' trust in the
oracle that he receives early in the play about the murderer(s) of Laius; ignoring his
trust in the oracle when he first visited Delphi from Corinth as a youth (*OT* 796f);
and ignoring the scrupulously correct and pious behavior of Oedipus in the opening
scenes (e.g., 66ff, 244f) and the reverence with which he is regarded by the priest
at 14ff. Overall, Oedipus does not markedly resemble "the person who scoffs at religion..."; and while Knox is right to conclude (p. 42 = A5c) that "The play is a terrifying affirmation of the truth of prophecy," his expansion of this into a condemnation
of Oedipus' behavior is not justified by the text. The incompatibility between A6 and
B3 can thus be resolved, since we can confidently discard A6 and the conclusions that
flow from it.

W. is right, then, to oppose Knox's over-simplified view of Oedipus' behavior
as "defiance of prophecy" and thus as "undermining of religion." (This is not to deny that these implications *are* present in Oedipus' actions and attitudes.) He is right
too to oppose the view of Oedipus' downfall as a straightforward demonstration of the
inadequacy of rational inquiry, and to emphasize the positive achievements of Oedipus
in his dauntless search for knowledge. But there are several points in W.'s own argument where I think he does less than justice to the text, and is thus led to conclusions about the message of the play which I should not accept.

(a) W. overstates the achievements of Oedipus' unaided intellect. We should not deny that the plague, the oracle received via Creon, and the chance arrival of the messenger from Corinth, all provide vital stimuli and information from outside Oedipus himself, without which he would never discover the truth. Of these three stimuli, the first two are clearly of divine origin (Apollo is god of disease; and after the *Iliad* it would be hard for any Greek audience not to see him as author of this one too; and it is he who explains how to remove it); and the third follows right after Iocasta's prayer to Apollo (919-923). Oedipus' discovery of the truth is thus a joint effort, human and divine.

(b) W. draws too simple an opposition between free, human will and divine determination (W. p. 9, p. 11; so too Knox, W. pp. 4ff). Since E. R. Dodds' *The Greeks and the Irrational* (Berkeley 1951) we have been accustomed to the idea of "double-determination," whereby the same event is presented as both divinely caused and humanly chosen; no contradiction is felt, and the problem of free-will is simply not acknowledged before the Stoics. Much of Knox's discussion, and some of W.'s (pp. 9ff) should, I think, be modified to take account of this way of seeing the world. It is a mistake to pin Sophocles down to a simple either/or position.

(c) W. denies "true knowledge" to Teiresias, and makes a distinction between two kinds of knowledge, intuitive and rational, emphasizing the latter (the kind possessed by Oedipus) as superior. I think that this is a red herring. I see little evidence in the text that this distinction is significant for the play: on the contrary, the imagery of light/darkness, sight/blindness, etc. which pervades the play is at its most evident in the scene between Oedipus and Teiresias. We are thus led to believe that the knowledge which the one lacks and the other possesses is essentially the same, regardless of its source. (Likewise, I think that W. rather exaggerates the stupidity and insensitivity of the chorus. I see no reason to doubt that by the end of the play they have finally caught up with Oedipus, and "know" what he knows in pretty much the same way--just as the audience does.)

(d) (This is my most important objection to interpretation B.) In concentrating on the suffering involved in Oedipus' acquisition of self-knowledge, and ignoring its further consequences, W. limits his interpretation of the play to its meaning *for Oedipus the individual*; and even here he gives a curiously low value to the possession of knowledge as a reward in itself. W. argues (p. 13) that Oedipus suffers more intensely at the end of the play than at the beginning, and suggests, "*OT* is preeminently a play that demonstrates the profound personal cost of inquiry." But this conclusion can be challenged on two scores: first, it implies that Oedipus is objectively "happier" (because suffering less) while he is living in ignorance of his parricide and incest, whereas I think that most people would regard it as more admirable, perhaps even more desirable (if not more pleasurable) to live miserably in the bright light of truth than to enjoy apparent prosperity amidst the fog of delusion (to maintain the imagery of the play). Oedipus can "see" at last by the end of the play; to that extent his position is undeniably raised, though his awareness of pain is certainly much greater too. Secondly, and more important, this conclusion ignores the plight of the rest of Thebes, and the substantial benefits that Oedipus' discovery of the truth has brought once again to his city. He has found and expelled the murderer, and thus rid the city of the plague that ravaged it at the beginning of the play. The chorus may be shocked and chastened by what they have seen happen to Oedipus; but they are now in a position to live much happier lives than they could as long as he remained ignorant.

Interpretations C and D require little discussion. Any interpretation (C) which focuses on Iocasta as much as on Oedipus himself runs into difficulties, in that she is obviously a subordinate character. Nor does her ultimate fate (incest and inglorious suicide) mark her out as "superior" to Oedipus. But, most basic of all, the play shows little sign of being interested in the difference between intuitive and rational acquisition of knowledge. As for D, we are here faced with what I described as a "solipsistic" view of the text, which may remain "true" for the reader (in this case with liberal use of the magic wand of irony, whereby things constantly mean their opposite), but are regarded by most other readers (and in this case by the author too, no doubt) as quite unfounded and perverse. It is perhaps impossible to disprove Vellacott's interpretation, if one accepts his premises as to how a dramatic text works. One can merely observe that there are more economical ways of explaining that text; and that none of the thousands of readers and spectators who have preceded him (from Aristotle onwards) have managed to grasp what Sophocles "intended" according to his reading.

Of W.'s models in Section V, then, I tend to favor the first tetradic of p. 20, though I think that the second tetradic of p. 20 (including reference to authorial intention) is sometimes of value too (less so in the case of drama than in, e.g., lyric, novel, parable, sermon, etc.). I have no quarrel with W.'s characterization of most literary (and presumably biblical, philosophical, etc., too) interpretation as being argumentative, though I think that this has been recognized more widely than he implies. Certainly we should take note of the *rhetoric* of interpretation--though critics will vary widely as to the extent to which they take account of previous interpretations, or simply assert their own, baldly and as if no other view was even conceivable.

So what "direction" should we be taking, finally, as we look for an answer to the question, "What does *OT* mean?"? (W. p. 28) I think that I am at one with W. in concluding that we should ask questions of the text (questions more specific, I have suggested, than "What does it mean?", *tout court*), and hope to come up with answers that are (a) consistent with the text itself, (b) consistent with our personal response to reading that text (and with the responses of others known to us), and (c) consistent with attitudes and conventions of the original audience (and author), in so far as these can be ascertained. If (b) and (c) do not coincide, we should not be too surprised or put out. If (a) and (b) do not, we are probably misreading the text, or bringing false preconceptions to it of our own. If (a) and (c) do not, then our understanding of one of them is probably deficient--unless the author has unconsciously transcended himself and his age.

In this response, I have tried to dismiss interpretations A, B, C, and D on various grounds as not being simultaneously true to the text of *OT* and contradictory to each other. But I have not resolved W.'s main point, here or in my own mind, i.e., the principle, whether certain texts *may* admit of contradictory answers to the same question. Can someone come up with a particular question to ask of *OT*, to which two incompatible, but true, answers can be given?

---

[7]E.g., in the practice and theory of the Sophists (5th Century B.C.), who spent much time and energy disputing the meaning of famous poems, and claiming the superiority of their own interpretations. See Plato *Ion, Protagoras, Lesser Hippias*, etc.

MINUTES OF THE COLLOQUY OF 25 MAY 1980
List of Participants

Professor at *York University, Ontario, Canada*

Barrie A. Wilson *(Philosophy)*

Professors at the *University of California, Berkeley*

William S. Anderson *(Classics and Comparative Literature)*
John S. Coolidge *(English)*
Joseph Fontenrose *(Classics, Emeritus)*
Mark Griffith *(Classics)*
James Jarrett *(Philosophy of Education)*
Anitra Bingham Kolenkow *(Lecturer, Religious Studies)*
Thomas G. Rosenmeyer *(Classics and Comparative Literature)*
Raphael Sealey *(History)*
Gunther Stent *(Molecular Biology)*

Professors at the *Graduate Theological Union*

Marvin E. Brown *(Lecturer, Religion and Society)*
Michael Cook *(Systematic Theology)*
Edward C. Hobbs *(Theology and Hermeneutics)*
Ted Peters *(Systematic Theology)*
David Winston *(Hellenistic and Judaic Studies)*
William Wuellner *(New Testament)*

Professor at *Pacific Union College, Angwin, California*

Fred Veltman *(New Testament, Hermeneutics)*

Professor at the *University of California, Davis*

Irene Lawrence *(Lecturer, Religious Studies)*

Professors at the *University of the Ruhr, Bochum, West Germany*

Hans Gumbrecht *(Romance Literature)*
Peter Spangenberg *(Romance Literature)*

Professor at *Western Illinois University*

L. Bryant Keeling *(Philosophy)*

Guest

John L. Bogart *(New Testament)*

Students

Sharon Boucher *(GTU)*
Michael C. Schoenfeldt *(UCB)*

MINUTES OF THE COLLOQUY OF 25 MAY 1980

THE DISCUSSION

Summarized by Irene Lawrence

<u>Wilson</u>: I take my job as a philosopher seriously, to be an *agent provacateur*, and I will begin with these few remarks.

The situation that confronts hermeneutics is very much like the situation before Hegel's budding metaphysician who is advised that if he wishes to learn how to swim, not to seek prior epistemological justification for swimming, but to jump in and swim. One learns about interpretation by interpreting and by reflecting on interpreting. Put another way, the situation is very much like that which Wittgenstein says is before philosophy: to show the fly the way out of the bottle. Much conceptual clarification remains to be done if we are to understand the hermeneutic vectors within which we are situated. In a sense, however, both Hegel and Wittgenstein are unduly optimistic in supposing that there is a shore to which the metaphysician can swim or a way out towards which the philosopher can help the fly make his way. For within hermeneutics there is no such safe terrain or exit, no vantage point outside the hermeneutic circle from which to survey the territory.

Yet within the hermeneutic circle there is a square, or marketplace-- the square of controversy in which hermeneutic transactions of various sorts take place. In my paper I draw attention to several generally ignored features of this square. By way of response to my interpreters and critics, I will recapitulate a portion of the main argument my paper presents, and, in so doing, I will respond very generally to the many kinds of issues that the respondents have raised with respect to each point.

A portion of my main argument went essentially as follows. First of all, I point out that at least for some texts, when we ask what does it mean? we receive as an answer that it means this, or this, or this [t means i_1, i_2, i_3, etc.]. That is, some texts have multiple interpretations. Texts scholars examine are typically of this sort. Here I wish to make explicit, in response to one of Hans Gumbrecht's queries, that I am concerned only with the scholarly interpretation of texts. I am not advancing a general theory of *Verstehen*, nor an account which necessarily includes any ordinary non-scholarly sense-making of texts, nor indeed an account which embraces non-textual objects of interpretation (e.g., events, natural and social scientific phenomena, non-textual works of art, etc.).

Virtually any studied text allows for multiple interpretations. I took four differing interpretations of *Oedipus Tyrannus* and I am grateful to Joseph Fontenrose for developing a fifth one and for mentioning others. I think, too, with some modifications along the lines suggested by Joseph Fontenrose and by Mark Griffith that interpretation B still stands as a strong candidate as to the play's meaning.

Much the same point could have been made with respect to other texts-- e.g., the various interpretations of Shakespeare's *Hamlet* that Morris Weitz has examined for meta-interpretive purposes, the richness of parable interpretation emanating from contemporary parable scholarship, the perennial debate over Aristotle's talk of the separability of the active intellect in *De Anima*, and so on.

Secondly, I suggest that when we survey the multiple interpretations texts have received, we note that some interpretations are in some respects incompatible with other interpretations. This was and is the case between interpretations A and B (for, *pace* Mark Griffith, two interpretations may be incompatible, even if both should turn out to be false). It is also the case between the interpretation offered by Joseph Fontenrose on the one hand and Waldock and Vaughan on the other who reject any attempt to find meaning in *Oedipus Tyrannus*.

Incompatibility is the tough case, for with incompatibility it cannot be the case that both are true (although, of course, one may be true, or both false). This is somewhat of a contentious point in the literature on the logic of incompatible interpretations. Margolis, for instance, noting the critical tolerance of works of art contends that "...given the goal of interpretation, we do not understand that an admissible account necessarily precludes all others incompatible with itself."[1] This meta-interpretive tolerability of incompatibles is advanced by Margolis (and others) chiefly, I think, because they assimilate or at least group texts with other kinds of works of art. There is a crucial difference, however, between the non-absurdity of claiming that in the *Republic* Plato advances a notion of reincarnation or of maintaining that in *Oedipus Tyrannus* Sophocles is contributing to a discussion concerning the role of religion in society and the absurdity of contending that Mozart's *Die Zauberflöte* is about a custody suit or about the triumph of freemasonry. Works of art differ in kind and in what may be said about them by way of interpretation. Also if Margolis does not mean by "incompatible" that which cannot both be true, then it is difficult to discern what he could possibly mean by the tolerability of *incompatibles*. Beardsley is more on the right track, I would maintain, with his principle of the intolerability of incompatibles.[2]

As I say, incompatibility is the touch case, for here we must choose. But even interpretive diversity raises immense problems. I do not "deplore" such diversity, as Bryant Keeling puts it, but I am somewhat sceptical of what is alleged to follow from a statement that interpretations of texts differ. There are, of course, many reasons that have been cited to support the

[1] Joseph Margolis, "The Logic of Interpretation," in J. Margolis, *The Language of Art and Art Criticism* (Detroit: Wayne State University Press, 1965) 92.

[2] Beardsley maintains the following: "The issue between Margolis and myself, then, can be stated in this way: he holds that all interpretations have what he calls a 'logical weakness,' i.e., they tolerate each other even when they are incompatible. In contradiction to this view, I hold that there are a great many interpretations which obey what might be called the principle of 'the Intolerability of Incompatibles,' i.e., if two of them are logically incompatible, they cannot both be true." Monroe C. Beardsley, *The Possibility of Criticism* (Detroit: Wayne State University Press, 1970) 44.

inevitability of interpretive diversity, truths (or alleged truths) about the nature of texts, interpreters, interpretation, meaning, etc. If what follows from these is simply a statement that texts must therefore be viewed as having a catalog of interpretations, then I am somewhat sceptical of this alleged consequence. I would contend that on this understanding, (1) it would be difficult to avoid a solipsistic view of interpretation, (2) that it would abdicate the responsibility of critically evaluating interpretive positions, and (3) that it is false to the sort of interpretive practice in which scholars seek to establish an interpretation while eliminating others.

Thirdly, I suggest that we ought to pay close attention to one significant but neglected facet of textual interpretation, namely its disputative character, that is, that when an interpreter puts forward an interpretation, he characteristically does the following: (a) he denies the truth of rival interpretations--*vide* interpretive arguments A, B, C by implication, D, and Joseph Fontenrose's interpretive argument, and (b) he presents reasons to back up his interpretive claim that a text means such-and-such. I take this to be characteristic of what interpreters do when they work out an interpretive position.

Finally, I suggest, therefore, that the form textual interpretation takes is that of argumentation and that this represents a useful shift in meta-interpretive direction. Several points need clarification here. For one thing, in saying that interpretation takes the form of argumentation I mean, in response to Bryant Keeling, argument in a narrow, traditional sense, as involving premises, conclusion, and support for premises. This does not entail that all interpreters are or need to be logicians--just that their establishing an interpretive position involves an ordered line of reasoning in which interpretive reasons support interpretive conclusions. Nor does it restrict the sorts of considerations that can be introduced as premises. Nor does it mean, as Marvin Brown helpfully points out, that argument in interpretation is restricted to just arguments on behalf of interpretive conclusions.

Nor does this involve a neglect of the "for whom" an interpretation can be provided. Several of the respondents, notably Marvin Brown and Mark Griffith, have pointed out the role of the audience. I suppose I am advancing a narrower conception of interpretation than they. I certainly do not wish to deny that there are audiences for interpretations. But I do think it useful to distinguish between an interpretation and an adaptation or application of that interpretation. If, for example, I have worked out an interpretation of *Oedipus Tyrannus* that sees Oedipus portrayed as the suffering inquirer, I can then choose, as circumstances warrant, how to present this interpretation for purposes of, e.g., a classroom lecture, a scholarly forum, a sermon, a public talk, or even to modify my own lifestyle accordingly, etc., and in each case the presentation of that interpretation will differ. To include the "for whom" an interpretation is intended in with giving an interpretation of a text is to forfeit some useful hermeneutic distinctions.

There are many theoretical "tugs" in hermeneutics, e.g., to consider interpretation in relation to audience; to consider interpretation in relation to the interpreter's own preconceptions, interpretive frameworks, etc. in approaching a text; to consider interpretation in relation to text. My tugging is in the latter direction and in so doing I have sought to place focus on an aspect of hermeneutics on which focus is not now being placed.

Hobbs: The original paper and the critiques seem to raise three main issues,
which we have formulated as these questions:

(1) *Argumentative or disputative character of interpretation:*
Is it the case that the "conflict of interpretations" means that
interpretation is characteristically argumentation--pro i_x and con
i_y and i_z?

(2) *Incompatible interpretations:*
Is it the case that the existence of logically "incompatible" interpretations means that only *one* of them, or perhaps none, can be
"correct" (or "true")? Or, are texts (often) polysemantic?

(3) *Social character of interpretation:*
Is it the case that interpretation is intrinsically related to
the interpretative situation, to "social knowledge/communicative
competence," to audience/addressees/readers/spectators? (In Wilson's models, is the first "tetradic model" [p. 20] superior to
his "entadic model" [p. 21]?)

Coolidge: I would like to establish a distinction between "understanding,"
"interpretation," and "explication." Gadamer asserts a very close connection
between understanding and interpretation, that interpretation is the comple-
tion of understanding. Explication, then, would be the expressed, probably
written, validation of interpretation. Professor Wilson seems to be princi-
pally speaking of explication, which is characteristically argumentative. His
"interpretations," as Professor Griffith points out, tend to be propositions,
perhaps the "moral of the story," or "what it is about." But propositions are
not understanding, or interpretation, or explication. Such a proposition may
be regarded as an "axial statement," analogous to Hirsch's "intrinsic genre,"
which establishes an axis for determining what belongs to the meaning and what
is secondary. This effect is like that of Knox's presuppositions: some things
in the play come alive, some are merely inert, others are simply not seen. An
interpretative axis is a function of prejudice, as Gadamer points out. A rival
proposition establishes a competitive axis, and brings previously neglected
things into prominence. So incompatibility may not be a matter of logic, but
of competition between different axes of interpretation. Then the argumentative quality of interpretation pertains to the defense of an axis, rather
than to the interpretation itself.

Keeling: My observation of literary critics is that often they do not attempt
to put their work into rigorous argumentative form. They often simply describe, or call attention to things so that they may be seen. Professor Wilson
seems to be proposing a change in their procedures, and I would be interested
in hearing the grounds for this proposal; I do not think any have come up that
a literary critic would accept.

Gumbrecht: I assume there is no doubt that all scholarly interpretation involves argumentation. My question is whether textual evidence is, or should
be, the aim of argumentation. As an example, after World War II E. R. Cur-
tius wrote his famous book on Latin literature and European Middle Ages proposing a new attitude toward interpretation. The argumentative character of

the book was naturally not only related to the content of the interpretation but also to the approach. So we must differentiate between the different levels to which the argumentation is applied.

Wilson: Argumentation over the axis of interpretation can certainly take place at a variety of levels, including the meta-interpretive level. Certainly a Marxist, a Freudian, and a Catholic may not only arrive at different interpretations of a text, but may also argue over the appropriate axis. Clarification of the levels is crucial.

Hobbs: We are using "argumentation" in two senses. One sense is that interpretation is argumentative because it argues from premises to conclusions. The second sense is that interpretation is argumentative because it negates alternative points of view. Scholarly interpretation, of which Professor Wilson has been speaking, often does reject alternative interpretations, but several responses have spoken of interpretation as argumentative in the first sense, that it uses logic, and that the second sense might not always be the case. Interpretations do not always dispute, even when they are on the same axis.

Gumbrecht: To take an example, a Freudian interpretation would see sexual symbols throughout the text. Perhaps Professor Wilson would like to deny such an interpretation. By what type of argument can one deny that interpretation? Because it is not in the text? Because the interpretation makes no sense? Because it is dangerous to little children?

Wilson: If one wishes to approach a text with a particular perspective, such as Freudian--or Marxist, or Catholic--that would also be a premise, functioning within the argument, and would need defense.

Gumbrecht: But what kind of argument could be used to defend it? That the text demands it? That our situation demands it?

Brown: It is not possible to have anything other than a particular perspective, whether it is labeled (like "Marxist") or not. We are all caught in some particular perspective. The problem exists on the meta-interpretive level of somehow moving toward agreement, but that does not come from the evidence of the text, but from the audience. It may be a problem because of the lack of a universal audience.

Jarrett: Papers at the American Philosophical Association meetings tend to emphasize some one kind of argumentation so as to disqualify, for example, Nietzsche and Kierkegaard from being philosophers--their discourse was not in the acceptable mode. Might we be doing that here? Would we want to accept as a serious question the affective response that a given passage in *Oedipus Tyrannus* has on the audience? This is a response, and it makes a great difference in the meaning.

Stent: The answer to the first question proposed for our discussion seems to be critically dependent on the answer to the second. If the concept of "truth" is applicable to interpretation, then an interpreter would have to support his interpretation by arguments. But if the concept of truth need not apply, then an interpreter need only state what the text means to him, since an alternative interpretation would not necessarily be a rival to his own.

Rosenmeyer: As a reader, and as one who is fond of interpretations and holds some, I usually prefer an interpretation that is as little disputative as possible. We all know the range from the disputative doctoral dissertation to something very low in disputation such as Auerbach's *Mimesis*. It is conceivable that one may have an interpretation that does not wear any disputative quality on its sleeve.

Brown: "Conflict of interpretations" is Ricoeur's phrase, and he provides a different model of the conflict, not simply that one interpretation is right. He places each kind of prejudice and methodology in its proper place in the hermeneutical circle. Structuralism, for example, has a very useful function in the interpretation of texts, but it is inadequate by itself.

Wilson: I have two comments on this discussion of the first question. First, by pointing out the disputative character of interpretation, one can rule out "bizarre" hermeneutics, of which there are many forms, all characterized by the divorce of interpretive theory from interpretive practice. Historically, the paradigm case was logical positivism; Hirsch is another example. Interpretive theory should always be related to practice.

Secondly, interpreters do give reasons for the positions they advance. To raise questions about the breadth of the word "argumentation" is to misfocus the issue. Certainly very few interpreters set out arguments in the manner of a philosopher; it is the business of the philosopher--among other things--to set out arguments. However, within any interpretation one can find the pivotal statements. For example, Professor Fontenrose's interpretation has four main premises and a conclusion. That is characteristic of what interpreters do. This is not to limit the sorts of things that can count as premises, but to say that in all cases the premises need to be defended. By seeing them within the interpretive argument, they become manifest and open to defense; this is where the disputative character of interpretation lies.

Fontenrose: I raised the question of the first interpreter, who is not "disputing," but who makes an argument in the old sense of hypothesis. Of course, he may anticipate objections, but later interpreters dispute his and give another. Also, we should note that if a text were plain to begin with, it would not need any interpretation. One interprets, in the first place, because the text needs it.

Griffith: Turning to the second question, an example that I did not have space to discuss in my response is Kafka's parable toward the end of *The Trial*. A man approaches a gate, and is told to wait; he waits until the end of his life, and dies, and the gate remains closed. Four or five interpretations follow, described as coming from the "wise men of the community";

they are all incompatible and all are well supported. It seems obvious that Kafka did not intend for there to be one correct interpretation. Can we allow that all five of them are potentially true, but not necessarily true? How could we develop that?

Hobbs: The same issue was raised at our last meeting on Spenser, who offers us interpretations in the voice of E. K., which are not necessarily true. Certainly they are not Spenser, yet they are not necessarily false. In the case of *Vor dem Gesetz*, Kafka's intention is hermeneutical in offering us this diversity of interpretations, but surely not to lead us to yet another, single "correct" interpretation.

Another example Professor Wilson used is Gospel parable interpretation of recent years. There is probably more interpretive history on the parables than on anything else in Western literature. Of course, there are fashions; and a new fashion always seems to show how stupid the previous fashion was. But later it turns out that there was some merit in the previous method, too. For example, nineteenth-century commentaries were all allegorical, following many resources in the patristic period, especially in Alexandria. Yet the new work by Jülicher said that we must find a *single* point in a parable; they are *never* allegorical. But to whom? The Evangelists themselves give allegorical interpretations. Do we look for the mind of Jesus? The work of some who call themselves Structuralists provides a remarkable series of interpretations which are perhaps not incompatible but are at least so different as to seem incompatible. If we grant very different interpretations, yet apparently about the same issue, then both the history of and the contemporary scene in parable interpretation show that the parables are polysemantic. They are rich in evocative power, and stimulate a variety of interpretations not necessarily exclusive of each other. They seem to have a single deep structure which provides a great variety of surface structures which on the face of it are extremely diverse.

Gumbrecht: Any text taken as just text, out of its context, is polysemantic. The problem of incompatibility of interpretation arises when referring to a situation. There are indeed many different interpretations of the parables. But for example, in the Roman Catholic Church with its claim of meta-historical stability of interpretation, a number of different interpretations must raise the question of incompatibility. So we must define the situation before we can speak of incompatibility.

Coolidge: "Polysemantic" by itself is a blank check. Unless we want to allow every reader to make up his own poem, we need to say more. We may have many, even unlimited, possibilities, but a work is nevertheless determinate in meaning.

Stent: How can the concept of "truth" be applicable to textual interpretation? One possibility would be that an interpretation is "true" if it has captured the author's conscious intent. So one could ask the author, if he were alive, "Did you mean such-and-such?" But unfortunately a text is at least partially determined by the subconscious, of which the author is not usually aware, and the intent of which can easily be paradoxical.

Rosenmeyer: To say that a text is polysemantic does not mean that it can have any meaning whatsoever. It must be determinate in some sense, unless we give up all notion of a text as a stable unit. Then it is possible for two interpretations to be incompatible with one another.

Winston: I think we should make a distinction here. If the author intentionally wishes to mystify the audience, we have a special kind of work, such as Kafka's. But in most literary texts, the difficulty of determining the "true" interpretation is that we must learn it by indirection. For example, in Plato the enormous variety of interpretations is due to the fact that he does not use expository or philosophical essays, but the dramatic form. People read the dialog, and are unable to determine exactly what Plato's position is. That makes the work polysemantic.

Hobbs: "Polysemantic" does not mean that a text can mean *anything*; it means that there may be many--at least more than one--possible meanings. The weasel term that drives us to the notion that there is *only* one is "correct" or "true." This drives us to the *author's* intention, or an equivalent such as the mind of God. (I think this has been exploded; I hope there are no Hirschians here!) But for an interpretation to be meaningful or useful, to function significantly in a given time or situation, is a very different question. A Marxist interpretation, for example, might be very meaningful in a Marxist community, but the College of Cardinals would probably not find it very helpful, and might describe it, from their point of view, as "incorrect." But that is not appropriate terminology. The critics' real issue is, if there be a "correct" interpretation, are we driven to the view that the text cannot have alternate meanings?

Griffith: There are different sorts of texts, but most literary works are not "intended" to have a single meaning. Kafka trying to mystify us is an extreme example, but not a unique one, of what most poets and playwrights are doing. On the other hand, for a preacher or teacher interpreting a parable, it may be that the author's intentions are extremely relevant. I imagine that most Christians would like to be able to ask Jesus what he intended by a parable, and would consider that paraphrase or moral the best interpretation.

In the case of a philosopher writing in a literary mode--Plato is the perfect example--the problems that that creates must have been intended. Plato apparently thought that an expository text was not the best way to teach the truths he intended.

Gumbrecht: There is a kind of intercultural discussion, just the same in Western Germany as here, which one could call "Who's afraid of the polysemantic character of texts?" But this threat is not acceptable. A text must be read by someone to assume sense; the meaning is not "in the text." The Anglo-Saxon way of formulating "The text means. . ." is very strange; no one would say "The house means...." Regarding the "truth" of interpretation, there is also an Anglo-Saxon tradition, now fashionable, called the consensus theory of truth. One can say that an interpretation is true for a community of people who have to do with that interpretation; it might not be true for all--a Marxist interpretation in certain areas of Rome, for example.

Stent: It is no accident that the more obvious, or unambiguous, the meaning, the lower the literary merit that is generally attributed to a text. Compare La Fontaine with Kafka, for example.

Rosenmeyer: Perhaps Professor Gumbrecht exaggerates the fear of anarchy. I agree that our literature is polysemantic, but I feel strongly that the "poly" has to be confined rather narrowly, and we must work within limits. The fact that literature "means" something, while houses don't simply sets literature apart as something quite unusual. I suppose "means" here is a translation of the Greek *legei*, says, and that is not so strange. Literature is not ordinary discourse.

Coolidge: I would contest the statement that La Fontaine is inferior literature or negligible, just because it is, in form, the kind of fable which ends with a moral. That seems to illustrate what I began with: the moral is not the interpretation of the story, even when the genre claims it is.

Hobbs: Even if it were feasible to ask Jesus what he meant, it is striking that the early Christian community decided in effect that Jesus's teaching and action were polysemantic. What became authoritative for all succeeding interpretations were *four* Gospels, very different, and one of them virtually incompatible. Here was a hermeneutical community with a tradition of explicitly polysemantic interpretation from the very beginning. That did not mean that *any* interpretation was allowable. During the Middle Ages, following Jewish exegesis, the four-fold method prevailed, with occasional simpleminded theories--"God revealed the meaning to me"--intervening. But in the main, the Christian tradition began with the canonization of four Gospels and the discarding of the notion of a univocal message of Jesus.

Wuellner: It generated also a variety of ecclesial communities.[3]

Gumbrecht: Of course the canonization process excluded some texts, too. Then we must speak of the normative implications of a hermeneutical community. For my information: what arguments were used to exclude some texts and accept others?

Hobbs: They gave a bogus argument; they said the texts were "accepted everywhere always by all." Yet Gnostic communities clearly had other documents, recently discovered at Nag Hammadi. But the bulk of Christians decided that the Gnostics weren't Christian. So the Christians didn't say "Anything goes." They said, "*These* texts go, because they are accepted everywhere always by everyone."

Coolidge: But they said those four Gospels were one.

----

[3]In previous discussions of our center colloquies it was argued with reference to the work of Georges Dumézil (See Protocol #25, p. 90), that social transformations go hand in hand with linguistic, literary, and conceptual transformations. Cf. also E. P. Sanders, *Paul and Palestinian Judaism* (Philadelphia 1977) about "patterns of religion" in first-century Judaism . and Christianity.

Hobbs: Yes, but as with the Trinity, the "one" was curious.

Winston: An extreme case would be the Lurianic Kabbalah, which taught that every verse of the Torah has 600,000 aspects and meanings.[4] That is, one for the soul of each person who stood at the foot of Sinai. The rabbis had said that there were seventy aspects (*Numbers Rabbah* 13.15).

Fontenrose: There may be a difference between the meaning of *Oedipus Tyrannus* and the interpretations of it. Sophocles had a meaning or meanings, but his meaning couldn't possibly be the Marxist, or the Freudian, or the Catholic interpretation. Those are applied today, and take in considerations that lie outside the play. And of course there is more than one Marxist or Freudian interpretation. In my response, I was trying to get to Sophocles' own meaning, and the meaning of the tragedy.

Rosenmeyer: Professor Hobbs ruled Hirsch out of court. But when we consider great works of literature, are we not driven to think of the writers also? It is a literate and literary experience to want to integrate an author's personality into what we read; we are dissatisfied with anonymous texts. There is something about our reading that makes the reconstruction of intention attractive.

Stent: Do you think Sophocles *knew* what his meaning was?

Fontenrose: I think so.

Cook: The four Gospels bring us back to the question of incompatibility. The Gospel of John was not accepted for a long time because it was suspected of Gnosticism. Thus there was a frame of reference in which Gnosticism, or at least certain forms of it, were not acceptable. So the four did have to be somehow compatible; they could be polysemantic, but not radically incompatible.

If Jesus came back and we asked him to explain a parable, his answer would be another parable. He deliberately chose a polysemantic literary form because it involves the listener. The same is true of the Gospels. They are not simply an objective literary phenomenon in the first century, but they have to be heard in each age, and they have that power because they are a literary creation, not a philosophical or scientific statement about the way things are.

Hobbs: Among those dealing with interpretation as such (not just doing interpretation), I think Hirsch's work has been generally rejected. Of course, that does not prove he is wrong. But I think the apparent naturalness of our going to the question of the author's intention is a very modern phenomenon; it is less than two centuries old. More recently, it has been questioned. For example, Paul Ricoeur has pointed out that the invention of writing, then literature, created a new possibility: the release of a text from its author. As soon as an author issues a text, it has its own life, and his intentions have little or nothing to do with it from that point on. Even if we could ask

---

[4] Isaac Luria, *Seter ha-Kavvanoth* (Venice 1620): 53b.

him, he probably would not know. By "intention" we usually mean more than
what is conscious; we mean the author's entire intent, as we can reconstruct
it. But that does not differ from reconstructing the intent of the text.

Jarrett: I wonder if the author's intent is clear before its expression, or
only after the expression has made public the event of the text itself, which
is therefore open to the interpretations of others. This includes cases of
alleged mystification such as Kafka. It seems likely that the intention of a
Kafka in presenting a paradoxical situation is more than simply to mystify or
obfuscate. Rather, it is likely to be an attempt to reach beyond the paradox
to something for which the expresser himself has no explicit answer, involving others in the process of reaching out for an answer that is not yet clear
to anyone. It may be that the expresser offers a parable as a way of elicit-
ing further hermeneutical effort to reach toward a new synthesis that perhaps
lies always over the horizon.

Wilson: I would raise two questions about what has been discussed in this
section of the meeting. First, what is wrong with the College of Cardinals
that they do not understand the Marxist interpretation of the parables? It
seems clear that the parable of the Good Samaritan is about a mugging, and
an appropriate response would be to set up social agencies in Jericho! Second, can we afford polysemy? Certainly where there is intentional ambiguity
one cannot decide between incompatible interpretations. But there are cases
of questionable intentional ambiguity, as with the parables; in fact, when I
was devising this paper, I was not sure whether to take on the classicists or
the New Testament scholars. It is not clear whether Jesus came to mystify or
to clarify. I am interested in the meta-interpretive argument that John Dominic Crossan presents in *In Parables*. According to my philosophical reconstruction, he has three premises and a conclusion: first, that parables are not
allegory; second, that Jesus's parables function as metaphors; third, that the
metaphors are open-ended in that they confront the future and tease the mind
into active thought. The conclusion is that therefore the parables themselves
are open-ended. The interesting premise is the second: to what extent do
parables function as metaphors? I have seen discussion about the open-ended
function of metaphors, and I would not disagree with that; someone who writes
a metaphor is being intentionally ambiguous. But what entitles us to classify
parables as metaphors? This is not much defended in parable scholarship today.

One final observation: one of the most interesting theories of polysemy
in the history of interpretation has been the allegorical approach. It has
fallen on hard times since Jülicher denied that parables are allegories,
largely because allegories piled confusion on confusion. But the sources
of allegorical hermeneutics—for example, Origen, John Cassion, and Augus-
tine—propose different levels of meaning, but never suggest, either in theory or practice, that a text is polysemous at each level. As the allegorical
hermeneutical tradition developed, it began to appreciate an interdependency
among the hierarchy of meanings. In the beginning of the *Summa*, Thomas Aqui-
nas responds to an objection that a multiplicity of senses would produce an
undesirable confusion in Biblical and doctrinal exegesis. He answers that
among the levels of meaning the literal and historical meaning is primary,
and the others can be derived from it.

Griffith: My observation bridges questions two and three, and is still about a parable, the one in Hesiod's *Works and Days* which I mention in my response. I suppose it is the oldest parable, or animal fable, in Western literature. As it stands, we cannot dispute that it is polysemantic, but it does seem that Hesiod intended it to have one primary, correct, meaning, and he intended the other possible meanings only for those who miss the point. The context of the rest of the poem and knowledge of the audience give us the clues to the primary meaning, but it cannot be resolved within the parable itself. I suspect that with Jesus's parables also, the context in which he gave them and the rest of his teaching might give us a clue as to what he is likely to have meant. Of course a parable or animal fable in moral or religious teaching is very different from the writing of a drama.

Brown: Professor Wilson's earlier remarks separated one's interpretation of a text from its subsequent application to an audience. Gadamer has argued against that position, saying that the application is at the very center of hermeneutics, and does not come after one understands a text. I used legal hermeneutics in my own response to show that how one sees the audience determines how one understands the text. In the last decade or so, Biblical hermeneutics shows this even more clearly. New audiences have led to new understandings in feminist theology and liberation or third-world theology, with their audiences of women and the oppressed. For example, Jesus has been seen as a political revolutionary, and some scholars have seen the narratives as trying to mitigate the political implications. Of course this is debatable, but it does not involve first understanding the text and then taking it to some audience.

Keeling: There are texts, such as Skinner's *Walden Two*, which are very didactic and intend to make a point. But many important texts are not simply trying to say something that could be said in a direct way. They often intend to produce an insight, to get the reader to see things in a different way, to rearrange the furniture of his mind. Therefore the task of a critic is not just to put into words what the text means, but to put the reader in a better position to understand the text. If by his parables Jesus had simply intended to tell us some didactic truth, he probably would have done it more directly. This is to support the point that "truth" in texts is not always didactic, and therefore there is not one true interpretation, and to support the point that the critic must, because of his function, consider the audience. For example, the twentieth-century audience needs a lot of background for a first-century parable.

Rosenmeyer: I would go even further than Professor Griffith in his remarks on Hesiod. Even though apparently several interpretations of that parable are possible, only one can be right. I feel very confident in that particular case, because of the contextual situation and the genre. I would like to add "genre" to the formulation of question three. Just as the interpretation of a text is dependent on the social environment, so also a statement, or partial text, is dependent for its interpretation on the literary tradition of the genre.

Gumbrecht: Of course interpretation depends at least on the background of the person who is the interpreter. But there are two situations combined:

the scholar has his background knowledge, but there is also the possible
audience of the interpretation. Can we separate out the scholarly interpretation from the scholar's subsequent attempts to communicate to an audience? *Should* we separate them--the normative question--and *can* we? I assume the separation is a fiction. After World War II, German criticism
turned to New Criticism. Critics pretended to do this purely scholarly interpretation without any social involvement because of the overall historical
situation. We really are not able to separate the two, and if we could, we
should not.

Coolidge: The fact that a speaker or writer thinks in terms of an audience
and adjusts what he has to say in terms of that audience implies a conscious
distinction, at least a partial lack of identity, between himself and the
audience. That situation should be distinguished from that in which the
reader, without anyone else in mind, projects his and his community's prej-
udices onto what he is reading. A poor reading is one in which the reader's
understanding is simply imposed on the text. But when one has already read,
and understood, and interpreted any text, and then undertakes to explicate
it, at that point the rhetorical question is crucial. The *explication* is
determined by the audience, but the understanding is determined at a more
basic level by the community of interpretation, perhaps largely unconscious.

Brown: One can distinguish between wanting an audience to accept one's explication of the text, and wanting it to understand the text. Rhetoric may
make the audience think they are understanding the text, when they really
understand only one's understanding. I think the interpreter plays a different role; he changes the dynamics between the audience and the text.

Coolidge: I am persuaded of Gadamer's identification of understanding, interpretation, and application, but the distinction becomes very significant
with explication.

Gumbrecht: Of course explication is determined by the audience; but there
is not much use for scholarly interpretation that limits itself to trying
to communicate one's own interpretation clearly. Are scholars not obliged,
by ethics, to adapt their interpretation to the needs of the audience? We
do not take the role of "the text means such-and-such" but the role of one
who proposes acceptable, interesting, and rewarding interpretations.

Anderson: I would like to re-emphasize that the *Oedipus* is a play, not one
of the simpler forms of literature that we have mentioned. In the *Oedipus*,
all the cited interpretations stop when Oedipus discovers the truth about
himself. But the play goes on for another three hundred lines, with words
and music and applause. The audience was not focussing just on what Oedipus
did, but on what Sophocles did, to put together an aesthetic whole, with a
somewhat predictable structure. So we must think of a dramatic audience,
not us as readers, and we must distinguish between a propositional interpretation of what happened to Oedipus and the much more complex experience that
an audience actually has.

Wuellner: Are you thinking only of the performance that Sophocles had in mind
at that time and the medium of the stage performance, as historically and cul-
turally conditioned in Sophocles' society?

Anderson: I am trying to stress the special quality of drama.

Wuellner: Then the genre of the medium is also involved, for example, television, film, or stage.[5]

Hobbs: Unless it is taken as a purely historicist remark--that the meaning is only what it was in Athens just as the play left Sophocles' personal direction--Professor Anderson emphasized the third point: there is a setting which is part of the meaning of the text, even if the setting is a TV screen. I think the Gospels are as complex as plays, and in setting they were apparently originally read liturgically, probably as wholes. Then they also mean what they mean only in the setting of Christians gathered together to have Eucharist.

Wuellner: Then polysemantic requires the complement of "polypragmatic."[6]

Griffith: As Professor Gumbrecht mentioned, "means" is a dangerous word. Even *legei*, says, might lead to the intentional fallacy, as in "Sophocles says. . . ." The French would say "wants to say," as if the dramatist "wanted to say" something but was misled into writing a play instead. A playwright not only wants to say something, he wants to do something. Aristotle recognized that one thing a play does is affect the audience. I would insist that not all texts have to be interpreted with regard to the audience, but some do.

Fontenrose: Is Professor Anderson arguing that this is a well-constructed plot?

Anderson: I am saying that the plot continues beyond the point where Oedipus discovers the truth. There is another point: the dispute about what Aristotle considered the tragic effect--what happens to the central character, or what happens to the audience.

Wilson: I think a hidden issue has lurked in the background of this discussion: it is that interpretation has fundamentally to do with persons, most notably, the author, the audience, and the interpreter who mediates between the two. Much hermeneutical theory, these responses, and this discussion have paid attention to the persons involved. This presupposition has a particular thrust: if with old-fashioned semiotics we consider language to be concerned with syntax, semantics, and pragmatics, then interpretation under this presupposition has to do with pragmatics only, that is, with an interaction between persons. We might label this the "pragmatic presupposition."

---

[5] For an introduction and bibliography on the issues raised by this question about the choice of medium, see Helmut Schanze, *Medienkunde für Literaturwissenschaftler* (Munich 1974).

[6]This notion is explored by several writers in the collection of essays entitled and introduced by J. V. Harari, *Textual Strategies: Perspectives in Post-Structuralist Criticism* (Ithaca, New York 1979).

It was one of the turning points in hermeneutics when Schleiermacher drew attention, in the "divinatory moment," to the interpreter coming into "communion" with the author. It is to be found in Dilthey's category of inner and outer which expresses the interpreter's *Verstehen* of the author. It is to be found in Heidegger's ontology of human being.

It is, however, a presupposition that has to be seriously questioned, and I have tried to do that. I think there have been some interesting reversals of this presupposition. For twenty-five years or so within hermeneutics there have been discussions about the role of the author, his intended meaning, and whether "communing" with the author is necessary. A consensus seems to have been reached that the object of our interpretation is the text, not the author personally, and it is not a requirement that we understand the author personally in order to understand the text. The thrust of this discussion has been to remove the focus from the author onto the text. That is not to say that all information about the author is irrelevant; for particular texts, considerations about the author might be warranted, but one would have to argue for it. This removes one of the persons from this constellation that the pragmatic presupposition puts before us.

The same thing can be extended to the other persons. The interpretive framework an interpreter brings to bear on a text is important, as well as the "for whom" the text is interpreted. However, these considerations will come out in the interpretation given to the text. Just as considerations about the author manifest themselves *in the text* he has written, so considerations about the interpreter and the audience manifest themselves *in the interpretation*. This leaves us with one text compared with another: the interpreting text and the interpreted text. This line of thought will undo the pragmatic presupposition, and we will move away from the whole area of pragmatics back into the area of semantics, and perhaps even to syntax. At least it will put hermeneutical inquiry into a different level of focus with many unanswered questions, such as the relation of the interpreting text and the interpreted text.

63

SELECT BIBLIOGRAPHY OF BARRIE A. WILSON

"Bultmann's Hermeneutics: A Critical Examination," *Internat. Jr. for Philos. of Religion* 8 (1977) 169-89.

"Hirsch's Hermeneutics: A Critical Examination," *Philosophy Today* 22 (1978) 20-33.

"Frege's Concept of Thought," *Studies in Language* 2 (1978), 87-101.

"Religious Language: The Language of Disobedience and Vision," *Sophia* 18 (1979) 10-17.

"Ecclesiological Models: An Epistemological Examination," *Encounter* 40 (1979) 327-39.

"What is Hermeneutics? An Introduction." The National Information and Resource Center for Teaching Philosophy, Fall, 1979.

"Interpretation: The One and the Many," *Queen's Quarterly* 87 (1980) 16-30.

Anatomy of Argument, forthcoming, Fall 1980, The University Press of America.